Cognitive Behavioral Therapy

A Comprehensive Guide to Using CBT to Overcome Depression, Anxiety, Intrusive Thoughts, and Rewiring Your Brain to Regain Control Over Your Emotions and Life

© **Copyright 2019**

All Rights Reserved. No part of this book may be reproduced in any form without permission in writing from the author. Reviewers may quote brief passages in reviews.

Disclaimer: No part of this publication may be reproduced or transmitted in any form or by any means, mechanical or electronic, including photocopying or recording, or by any information storage and retrieval system, or transmitted by email without permission in writing from the publisher.

While all attempts have been made to verify the information provided in this publication, neither the author nor the publisher assumes any responsibility for errors, omissions or contrary interpretations of the subject matter herein.

This book is for entertainment purposes only. The views expressed are those of the author alone, and should not be taken as expert instruction or commands. The reader is responsible for his or her own actions.

Adherence to all applicable laws and regulations, including international, federal, state and local laws governing professional licensing, business practices, advertising and all other aspects of doing business in the US, Canada, UK or any other jurisdiction is the sole responsibility of the purchaser or reader.

Neither the author nor the publisher assumes any responsibility or liability whatsoever on the behalf of the purchaser or reader of these materials. Any perceived slight of any individual or organization is purely unintentional.

Contents

INTRODUCTION 1

CHAPTER 1: THE BASIC PREMISE OF CBT AND HOW IT CAN BENEFIT YOU IN DAILY LIFE 3

CHAPTER 2: THE FASCINATING HISTORY OF CBT 13

CHAPTER 3: 16 COMMON MISTAKES AND MYTHS ABOUT CBT 18
    Common Myths *18*
    Common Mistakes *23*

CHAPTER 4: AN IN-DEPTH LOOK INTO WHAT CBT CAN TREAT AND WHY IT WORKS 29

CHAPTER 5: THE KEY PRINCIPLES OF COGNITIVE BEHAVIORAL THERAPY 45
    Thought Journaling *53*
    Fact-Checking *54*
    Cognitive Questioning *56*

CHAPTER 6: OVERCOMING ANXIETY AND DEPRESSION STEP-BY-STEP 58
    Week One *58*
    Week Two *65*
    Week Three *66*
    Week Four *69*

Week Five *70*

Week Six *72*

Week Seven *73*

Week Eight *75*

Week Nine *76*

Week Ten *78*

Week Eleven *81*

Week Twelve *82*

CHAPTER 7: 3 ALTERNATIVE CBT APPROACHES **86**

Mindfulness Therapy *86*

Acceptance and Commitment Therapy *87*

Dialectical Behavior Therapy *89*

CHAPTER 8: DISCOVER 7 INSPIRING TALES OF CBT SUCCESS **92**

Christine's Story *92*

Sarah's Story *95*

David's Story *99*

Joy's Story *100*

John's Story *101*

Tony's Story *101*

Tabitha's Story *102*

BONUS 1: EXERCISES AND POWERFUL AFFIRMATIONS TO REGAIN CONTROL OVER YOUR LIFE AND EMOTIONS **104**

BONUS 2: A PRACTICAL CBT WORKBOOK TO HELP YOU ACHIEVE YOUR GOALS **108**

Example: Thought and Behavior Cost/Benefit Analysis *109*

Thought and Behavior Cost/Benefit Analysis *111*

Example: Thought Record *113*

Thought Record *114*

CONCLUSION **115**

Introduction

Cognitive-behavioral therapy, otherwise known as "CBT," is an incredibly well-known therapy method within the field of psychology. Yet, unless you work within this field you likely know very little about CBT, how it works, and why it is one of the best therapy methods around. In this book you will learn about the amazing affects this therapy has been proven to have. You can learn how to use cognitive behavioral therapy from within your own home, helping to treat anxiety, depression, post-traumatic stress disorder, panic disorder, obsessive-compulsive disorder, and more. No longer do you have to suffer in silence, simply existing through life. You can learn to heal and begin to actually live a full life again. Whether you have been diagnosed with social anxiety disorder, major depression, post-traumatic stress disorder, or simply are struggling throughout your daily life without a diagnosis, CBT can help. While it is always best to go to a professional and receive a diagnosis of your condition, you can also use the tools of CBT independently at home, with or without an official diagnosis. You can learn to better understand your mind, overcome intrusive thoughts, cope with daily stress, and transform your negative thought patterns into something more positive. Cognitive-behavioral therapy is truly transformative, and with a little daily effort, you can change your entire life for the better.

By choosing to make a simple change in your life, taking one step forward a day at a time, you can use CBT for a better and more fulfilling life. Whether you are struggling under daily stress, numb from depression, or feeling panicked about various aspects of life, you can find healing. By working at it a little each day, you will find a brighter and better life than you ever imagined, all with the power of cognitive-behavioral therapy.

Chapter 1: The Basic Premise of CBT and how it Can Benefit You in Daily Life

Cognitive-behavioral therapy was developed during the 1960s by the hypothesis that more than a situation itself, it is how we view a situation that affects our feelings. For instance, if two people get into an argument, they may each experience vastly different feelings, even though they were both a part of the same situation. One individual may view the situation as a worst-case scenario, worrying that they have lost a friend and that they will never be able to resolve the argument. By viewing the situation in this way, the first individual will feel hopeless, depressed, and anxious.

On the other hand, while the second individual is also upset about the argument, they feel much more balanced emotions. Instead of feeling hopeless they feel hopeful that the situation can be remedied. Instead of feeling depressed and anxious, they feel stressed, but still have hope that their friendship will ensure, helping to keep the second individual calm. The second individual can feel calm and hopeful in spite of the stress of the argument because of how they view the situation. Unlike the first person, they don't view the situation as a worst-case scenario; instead they view it as a normal part of friendship and interaction. By keeping in mind that conflict is normal and can be dealt with, the second individual is better able to cope emotionally, thus allowing them to also handle the situation better.

These two individuals illustrate how during daily life the way we view our circumstances shapes our emotions. If you spill a glass of milk, you can view the situation in multiple ways. You can either view it as another failure in your life or you can view it as a simple slip up that's easily remedied. The way we view our everyday circumstances shapes our emotions and feelings, which then create habits that we continue to follow in the future. This is the most basic premise of cognitive-behavioral therapy or CBT.

How we view a situation, which leads to the development of our feelings, is known as the cognitive model. This model explains how our views are formed. By understanding this model, we can begin to change our views for the better, thereby positively affecting our worldview, emotions, and reactions. This cognitive model has three parts which are:

1. Core belief
2. Dysfunctional assumptions
3. Negative automatic thoughts

From these three aspects of the cognitive model, the core belief is what you begin with, which then leads to the development of dysfunctional assumptions and negative automatic thoughts, in turn. What are these core beliefs? Put simply, they are the beliefs we hold onto deeply without even realizing it. These beliefs were formed during our childhood, early life, and lived experiences and make up what we believe about the world, others, ourselves, and even the future. We unconsciously hold these thoughts to be absolute truth, unwavering in our belief.

Example of core beliefs includes believing *"I'm worthless"* about yourself, *"the world is cruel"* about the overall world and others, and *"nothing good will come"* about the future.

Our rigid and extreme beliefs are known as dysfunctional assumptions. These assumptions do not truly reflect reality; they are excessive and over-generalized. The problem with these assumptions is that they frequently get in the way of our goals and emotional well-being instead of promoting positive outcomes. Common themes for dysfunctional assumptions are categorized as being based on control, achievements, and acceptance. Some examples include thinking *"If I can't do it perfectly, then I might as well not do it at all." "If they dislike me then something must be wrong with me."* and *"It's a sign of weakness to ask for help."*

Negative automatic thoughts are the third and final phase of the cognitive model. While our core belief is usually subconscious - and we are usually unaware of our dysfunctional assumptions - negative automatic thoughts take place in our conscious mind. We are aware of these thoughts, even if we don't realize the harm that they are causing us. These thoughts are involuntary and are most negative in people with depression, anxiety, post-traumatic stress disorder, and obsessive-compulsive disorder. People with these disorders often think of a situation as more disastrous or harmful than is true and also underestimate their ability to cope with the situation. Thoughts such as *"I'm completely useless" "I made a mistake, now everything is ruined" "If I try I'll only fail, so what's the point" "If I don't get this job I'll never get one"* and *"Bad things always happen to me"* are all examples of negative automatic thoughts.

With cognitive behavioral therapy, the cognitive model of these three processes is used in order to understand a person's thoughts behind their emotions. If you can alter the initial thoughts and replace them with something better and more truthful, you can, in turn, change your feelings. For instance, if a person is feeling overwhelmed it might be because their core belief is *"If I can't do something perfectly then I might as well not try at all"* and their negative automatic thought could be *"I made a big mistake that can't be fixed"* - leading them to want to quit. In order to fix the feeling of being overwhelmed, the person can then deal with the actual problem, adjusting their thoughts to something more accurate and positive. This is much more effective in changing feelings than covering up your feelings with insincere platitudes.

There are many ways in which to address these core beliefs, dysfunctional assumptions, and negative automatic thoughts. With cognitive behavioral therapy, there are formulas that are used to treat various core beliefs. Various types of core beliefs are sorted into categories, and then formulas are created for each category. This enables a person to narrow down what category their individual core beliefs fit into, allowing them to then know which formula of CBT is best suited for therapy.

With cognitive behavioral therapy, a person is taught how to help themselves independently. Yes, many people are guided through the process of CBT by their therapist. Although, the basic principles of this therapy teach the individual how to help themselves, even without a therapist. This is great, as a person can get the help they need even if they are unable to see a professional for one reason or another. You can learn the knowledge and tools you need to correct your maladaptive thought and behavior patterns, creating room for something much healthier. If you are diligent and take small steps daily to correct your cognition, you can create a healthier and happier you.

When a therapist is using cognitive behavioral therapy with their patient, the two work together, hand-in-hand. The therapist will help their patient discover which of their cognitions and behaviors are maladaptive or harmful. Once they isolate specific cognitions, these will then be analyzed, tested for their validity, and then if they are deemed to be untrue or harmful - the therapist will help their patient make revisions. The purpose of this process is to help the patient learn how to identify and manage problems, allowing them to gain the skills to do this on their own so that the training wheels can come off, allowing the individual to excel independently.

Rather than focusing on the past or the future, as some forms of therapy do, cognitive-behavioral focuses on the here and now. Instead of taking a wandering path around your problems to find a solution, you can directly confront your problems and fix them to see real and solid results. If you are struggling to heal after a traumatic event or struggling with daily anxiety when faced with interacting with other people, you don't have to talk about your childhood or your dreams to fix your problems. The approach CBT takes is much more straight-forward. By knowing what is causing you problems your distorted cognition can be revealed, and once this distortion is made plain to see it can be changed for the better.

Often, when working on improving a problem, you will set goals for yourself to track improvement and help yourself know what might or might not be working. These goals should fit the SMART standard of being specific, measurable, achievable, relevant, and timely. Not all of these goals have to be big - most of them will be small baby steps - but having something specific to work toward will motivate and encourage you. These goals will be different for every person depending on their common obstacles and troubles. For instance, a person with a social anxiety disorder may have the goal to be able to talk to strangers, be more assertive, or perform on stage. Likewise, a person with the major depressive disorder might have the goals of reaching out to friends, getting out of the house, and opening up about their feelings. No matter your reason for choosing cognitive behavioral therapy, a core principle is setting SMART goals to help you move forward and make actionable and effective change. For this goal setting, a person will have to analyze themselves and decide what goals are important to them, what goals will help them recover. These goals aren't always easy, sometimes they are frightening, but you can start small and work your way up to the more difficult ones. Once you obtain your baby step goals, you can then create a new list of steps that make it a little further and further until you have obtained your overarching goal of a better life.

Cognitive-behavioral therapy is named thus as its purpose is to change how a person thinks, otherwise known as their cognition, and how they act, which is their behavior. To this end, CBT uses multiple techniques that pinpoint both the cognitive and the behavioral aspects of a person to direct change and growth. The exact techniques will vary from person to person and case by case, but many of the techniques that people use share similarities. These techniques can be slightly altered for the individual as they are highly versatile. We will go into these methods and techniques into great detail later on in this book. However, for the moment, let's look at brief synopses of some of the more prominent and popular techniques so that you can develop a good understanding of what will be used later on.

Journaling:

There are a couple of types of journaling that are frequently used in CBT. While some people may keep general journals to work through their emotions and circumstances, there is a specific thought journal that is vital to the therapy process. This thought journal catalogs thoughts and feelings, their intensity, how you reacted to them, what supports the thoughts or feelings, or disproves the thoughts or feelings, whether they were proven to be true or false, and new healthier thought. For instance, if your initial thought was that everyone must hate you, this thought will then be disproved and replaced with a more balanced and healthier thought. By keeping this journal, you can begin to recognize your negative thought patterns and slowly work on confronting them and replacing them with something healthier. It will take time, but it has been proven to be effective. While a regular journal isn't always used with CBT, it remains a vital part of the process; everyone is encouraged to keep one of these thought journals.

Cognitive Restructuring:

In order to restructure our cognition, we must first start by unraveling its distortions. To do this, we must become more intimately aware of ourselves, not hiding from who we are but truly allowing ourselves to see what distortions we are suffering from. Once we isolate these distortions and what they are, we begin to analyze how and why they were formed. Now that you understand this distortion, you can begin to challenge it, beginning the process of restructuring.

For instance, if you believe that you are worthless and are struggling to love yourself or treat yourself kindly, you will need to directly confront these feelings of worthlessness. Instead of uncritically accepting this idea that you are worthless, you will take some time to consider what makes a person either lack or hold worth. Once you have considered what true worth consists of, you can then see the many areas in which *you are* a worthwhile human being.

Exposure and Response Prevention:

This method may be used with some anxiety disorders, but the most common and effective use for this technique is in the treatment of obsessive-compulsive disorder, or OCD. Some people think of OCD is simply being a little too tidy, enjoying cleaning, or liking office supplies. The truth is that none of these are factors of OCD. This disorder is quite literally an obsession that a person feels compelled to act on. For instance, a person may feel that if they don't flick the light switch precisely ten times after entering a room that something dreadful will happen. They might not be able to say what will happen, but the intensity of the feelings is equal to as if the entire building were to explode if they don't act on the obsession. People have many types of OCD; sometimes it includes germs, but there are many other types where germs play no role in the person's obsession.

To treat OCD with cognitive behavioral therapy exposure and response, prevention is used as an effective technique. This technique should start small and gradually increase in intensity, as the person will be exposing themselves to their compulsive behaviors but will try to refrain *from acting on the behaviors*. This can be incredibly difficult, which is why the method should always use baby steps at a pace the person is comfortable with. Once an individual practices exposing themselves to a compulsion without responding to it, they may journal about the experience and how it made them feel. This can give them greater insight into their feelings, and it can help to reflect on in the future as they continue to work through later stages of this technique.

Play Out the Script:

This method is most frequently used for people who struggle with anxiety disorders or phobias, though it may also help people undergoing other types of stress and fear. With this technique, a person who is prone to debilitating anxiety or fear conducts a thought experiment allowing them to imagine possible worst-case scenarios. The person allows the script of the scenario to play all the way through, seeing that even if what they fear does occur, they will still be able to handle it.

This does not work with all types of fears, but there are many situations in which it is applicable. For instance, if a person is having anxiety about running late to an appointment, their test scores, or giving a speech - then this technique can help.

Progressive Muscle Relaxation:

If you are familiar with mindfulness practices, then you are likely also aware of progressive muscle relaxation. With this technique, a person focuses on relaxing one set of their muscles at a time, until all the muscles in their body are relaxed. You can either do this on your own or with audio guidance, and either sitting up in a chair or laying down, making it easy to practice whenever and wherever you need. This technique is great for helping soothe a hyperactive mind or calm nerves, making it a wonderful option for the treatment of people with anxiety disorders.

Breathing Exercises:

Along with the previous technique, this will be familiar to people who practice mindfulness or meditation. Breathing exercises are a wonderful way to relax. This technique uses controlled and timed breathing to forcefully relax the body and mind. You can practice this method either on your own or with audio to walk you through the process.

This technique can be helpful regardless of the diagnosis. It does not matter if you have depression, anxiety disorder, obsessive-compulsive disorder, or simple day-to-day stress.

Activity Scheduling:

With activity schedules, a person has scheduled pleasurable activities to enjoy, which is to help the person treat depression and anxiety by systematically increasing the number of pleasurable experiences. It may take time for a depressed person to enjoy their favorite activities again, but by increasing their frequency, the person will gradually improve. To do this, the person should have a list of pleasurable activities, and then every week they should set aside time within their schedule to complete at least one of these activities. Larger activities such as going to the movies may only occur once a week, whereas smaller activities like enjoying a favorite snack should be enjoyed daily. Over time, this process will increase the number of pleasurable experiences, establish a daily routine, and increase the person's problem-solving abilities.

Behavioral Experiments:

Often used with people struggling with anxiety disorders, behavioral experiments allow a person to overcome their catastrophic thinking and replace it with something much more realistic and balanced. For instance, if a person feels that if they start participating in a local support group, that something terrible will happen, the person will put it to the test. To do this, they will write out what their fear is, test out the hypothesis by completing the test and then evaluate it to see if their fear was true or not. This means that the person may try attending one of the meetings of the local support group, and then afterward they will assess if their fear of something terrible happening came true or not. With this technique, a person can overcome their anxiety and negativity.

There are many techniques involved in cognitive behavioral therapy. Not all of these techniques are required to be used by the same person, as the techniques needed will vary based on the person's individual condition. However, no matter which of the above techniques are needed, CBT has been proven time and again to be effective. Many studies and reviews have demonstrated this method of therapy to be constructive in the treatment of mental illnesses, such as depression or an anxiety disorder. In fact, it has been proven through multiple professional studies that a person is much less likely to experience a relapse in their depression over time if they use CBT as a therapy method.

Beginning with cognitive-behavioral therapy does not have to be difficult, you can easily learn how to adopt this amazing therapy for the better of both your present and future.

Chapter 2: The Fascinating History of CBT

Cognitive-behavioral therapy first took roots in behavioral therapy. At first, behavioral therapy was criticized as being an untested theory, creating much controversy in the field of psychotherapy. Yet, the proponents of this therapy persisted and proved that the methods it teaches were underestimated. In the early stages, one of the most well-known successful uses of behavioral therapy was in the treatment of children with enuresis, a condition causing them to lose control of their bladder. This use of behavioral therapy, among others, created empirically supported evidence leading to the widespread and accepted use of the therapy for many conditions. The use of targeting and addressing observable behaviors and then tracking the outcomes (an essential part of what would later become cognitive behavioral therapy), were being used at this time in behavioral therapy. By the 1960s, the clinical use of behavioral therapy had become much more widespread, creating more awareness and helpful techniques.

You have most likely heard of the scientist, Ivan Pavlov, most famous for the experiment Pavlov's Dog. In this experiment, Pavlov introduced a neutral stimuli source in the form of a bell ringing and paired it with the potent stimuli of food. After a short time of the bell ringing every time the dog was given the food, the dog began to unconsciously tie the two sources of stimuli together in its brain. Soon, every time the bell rang, the dog would begin to drool and desire food - even when no food was present.

Pavlov's experiment went well past training dogs, as it allowed scientists to find new ways to beneficially affect the human mind as well. One of the most powerful uses of Pavlov's experiment is in respondent conditioning used in therapy. While during the time of the production of this technique, cognitive behavioral therapy was still a thing of the future, respondent conditioning would be a central part of the therapy for many individuals with fears or anxieties.

With respondent conditioning, two sources of stimuli are introduced to a person, similar to the experiment with Pavlov's Dog. Although, in this case, the stimuli are of a conditioned fear response, such as a fear of bees, paired with the absence of unconditioned stimuli, meaning not getting stung. Therefore, therapists would help their patients interact with something such as bees that usually scared them, but in a safe environment where they would not get stung. Over time, the person's brain tied the two stimuli together until their fear lessened and they no longer believed that being close to bees would result in being stung. This can help people with many types of fears. For example, if a person is afraid of dogs, they might interact with calm and small dogs until they overcome their previously conditioned response. Many studies of respondent conditioning found this method successful, as it greatly reduced anxiety in those it treated.

Over time, behavioral therapy continued to develop more procedures that would later on become a part of cognitive-behavioral therapy. The researchers and therapists use behavioral therapy saw the importance of addressing a person's cognition and thought process in the course of treatment. These developments were made with people of all ages in mind, meaning that they were proven to be effective with adults and children alike.

Cognitive-behavioral therapy began to take root in behavioral therapy and self-talk therapy in the 1970s. During this time, two of the earliest uses of cognitive-behavioral therapy -combining the previously accepted approaches - was utilized to help children. The therapists helping these children trained them how to use positive self-talk, coping mechanisms, and other common techniques. In the treatment of these children, the therapists saw great promise in combining both the behavioral and cognitive therapies to create a new and better option. By combining the two approaches, the children were able to receive more effective and balanced treatment that truly targeted and fixed their problems.

Doctors A.W. Meyers and W.E. Craighead aided in creating the shift of incorporating cognitive understanding and techniques into behavioral therapy to create CBT. A large part of this shift was incorporating cognitive psychology when treating children with behavioral therapy. They introduced cognitive modeling, self-talk and instruction training, and problem-solving. With cognitive modeling, children were taught how they could learn based on observation, allowing them to learn how to act and respond to situations by watching the behavior of another person and modeling their reaction from that person. The modeling technique was a classic form of behavior therapy, but Meyers and Craighead focused on attention and retention, which were inspired by cognitive psychology.

A. Bandura acted as a springboard for the advancement of cognitive-behavioral therapy when he explained the connection between the cognition and behavioral changes. This led to more therapists and researchers to begin to understand and focus on the needed understanding of the human cognition and information processing for behavioral therapy, thereby advancing CBT.

Self-instruction training, a hallmark of behavioral therapy, was soon impacted by cognitive psychology, as well. Self-instruction training, which was originally developed to help impulsive children how to better control their behavior, improved with the understanding of cognitive psychology. It was found that self-instruction was more successful when self-talk was introduced. This helped children to learn how to better control their behavior by using phrases and affirmations that spurred on the type of behavior they were encouraged to act on.

Problem-solving from behavioral therapy is another aspect that was altered for CBT. With this technique, individuals would focus on their thought processes to help create change. After all, problem-solving while affecting behavior requires information processing, which is part of cognition. This was so successful that it spurred on the use of this technique as a means for creating positive changes in both behavior and cognition in therapy.

One of the core beliefs of cognitive-behavioral therapy is that maladaptive cognitive processes worsen psychological disorders, and can, therefore, be reduced by making changes to the cognitive processes. This belief and the success it brought for adults and children alike gave way to a rise of CBT so that it became widely understood and utilized.

Around this time, two proponents for CBT, R.A. Harper and A. Ellis, promoted their belief that maladaptive behaviors and negative moods are a result of maladaptive thinking patterns. Therefore, they argued that CBT should focus on changing and improving maladaptive thought processes in order to change maladaptive emotions and behaviors. They believed that misconceptions about oneself and the world are tied directly to psychological disorders. These beliefs have been proven correct time and again through the study and treatment of people with anxiety disorders, depression, bipolar disorder, post-traumatic stress disorder, and more. Research has shown that these early proponents for cognitive behavioral therapy were correct and that by focusing on the cognition of a person, we can change their thinking, emotions, and behaviors for the better.

With favorable research on their side, more techniques and strategies were gradually integrated into what was now known as cognitive-behavioral therapy. These various techniques proved to be effective in treating various disorders. Since not all psychological disorders are alike, it helped to have a variety of techniques that could be used and customized depending upon the patient's specific conditions and needs. For instance, this allowed people with a social anxiety disorder and bipolar disorder to both have treatments tailored to their specific needs. These techniques also added variety when needed regarding a patient's age. Therapists learned how these techniques could be used in ways to benefit both adults and children so that everyone could find help regardless of age.

While cognitive-behavioral therapy took root in both behavioral therapy and cognitive psychology, over time it grew into something of its own, unique and distinct from the other two methods. CBT developed new models and techniques that could be used specifically within this type of therapy. Now, cognitive behavioral therapy is known as one of the most effective forms of therapy in treating people with common psychological disorders and traumas. Whether this therapy is being utilized with the aid of a trained professional or alone at home, a person is given the tools to succeed and find a healthy cognition and happy life again.

Chapter 3: 16 Common Mistakes and Myths about CBT

While most therapists and others in the psychology field have a good understanding of cognitive-behavioral therapy, it is easy for the layperson to develop misunderstandings of the method due to commonly purported myths. Along with myths about CBT running around, there are also a few common mistakes people might make during the therapy process. Thankfully, CBT is a simple and straight-forward therapy to complete when you are prepared with the proper tools. However, it is still possible to make simple mistakes. In this chapter, you will learn the truth behind the myths and learn about the most common mistakes and how to avoid them. If you keep this chapter in mind, you can have great success with CBT.

Common Myths

These myths spread easily, as people who have only a small understanding of cognitive behavioral therapy might misunderstand what they have learned. However, as this person believes that they understand the matter, they begin to spread their misunderstanding that creates these common myths. Let's have a look at the most common myths and the true facts behind them.

Myth #1: CBT is a Rigid One-Size-Fits-All Approach

One of the beautiful aspects of CBT is that it is a fluid approach with many techniques that can be applied to a variety of disorders. While a person with depression will use one set of techniques, a person with post-traumatic stress disorder will use another set of techniques. While these two individuals will use two different types of techniques, they will also use a few of the same methods, such as journaling, to help restructure their cognition. The truth is that CBT is in no way rigid or one-size-fits-all. It is a highly customizable approach that can be altered depending on a person's diagnosis, age, and individual circumstances. This approach recognizes that every person is unique, and therefore require a unique and tailored approach.

Whenever a person sees a highly trained cognitive-behavioral therapist, this therapist should be able to tailor their treatment plan for their specific needs. A person can also customize their own plan if they are using this book without the help of a therapist. Of course, it is always advised to seek professional help.

Myth #2: CBT Only Focuses on Replacing Negativity with Positive Thinking

Cognitive-behavioral therapy focuses on restructuring the cognition to be more balanced and less negative. Although, this is different from positive thinking. With typical positive thinking, a person is simply saying something positive to cover up their negativity. For instance, the person may say "nothing is wrong, I'm happy," even though they just got bad news and are devastated. This type of insincere positive thinking is like trying to get rid of deadly mold in your house by simply painting over it. This does not fix the problem, it only coats it with a temporary distraction, which will likely lead to disastrous results later on.

Instead of covering up your life with insincere positivity, cognitive behavioral therapy teaches people to learn to see their lives as realistically as possible. This means that you see both the good and the bad, with neither overshadowing the other. Having balanced and realistic cognition allows you to enjoy the good and address and fix any problems.

Along with looking at the world and yourself more realistically, CBT also teaches people to think more flexibly. This means that if a person is feeling nervous about giving a speech in front of a crowd, they can think about the situation flexibly. If the individual told themselves "I WON'T MESS UP, SO I SHOULDN'T BE WORRIED", this will not help, as messing up is certainly possible. Instead, the person is taught to think about other perspectives. For instance, they can think "EVEN IF I MAKE A MISTAKE, I CAN STILL DO WELL AND SUCCEED."

Myth #3: CBT Ignores Emotions

Nothing could be further from the truth than to say that CBT ignores emotions. The truth is that emotions are a very important part of the therapy process, they are just handled with a different approach from other types of therapy. With CBT, instead of dealing with emotions on their own, they are dealt with hand-in-hand with a person's cognition. This is because cognition is what affects a person's thoughts, behaviors, and emotions. Therefore, if you want to deal with difficult and troublesome emotions you must first understand the cognition behind them.

Myth #4: CBT Ignores the Past and Childhood

This myth has some truth in it, but only partially. The truth is that CBT usually focuses on the here and now, the problems currently affecting a person. Yet, when needed, a therapist will look back at their patient's past and how that past may be affecting their cognition and causing problems in their current life. For instance, if a person is suffering from post-traumatic stress disorder, the therapist will look back to see what caused the trauma. If a person has a social anxiety disorder, the therapist may discuss situations in the past that might have triggered the fear of social interaction.

A person may be able to look back at their past and see how it has negatively altered their cognition, but this can only be done reliably by a trained therapist. The truth is that we are unable to look at our own pasts completely accurately, especially when trauma is involved. However, a therapist specializes in understanding these difficult pasts and traumas with the ability to learn how to restructure the cognition into a balanced and healthy manner.

Myth #5: CBT Only Treats the Symptoms, Not the Problem

Cognitive-behavioral therapy, by definition, treats a person as a whole without reducing them to a set list of symptoms. This is because before it can even treat symptoms, it must first change a person's cognition. As a person's cognition improves, the person will find themselves thinking in a more balanced way about the world around them, others, and themselves. This, in turn, creates a change to the person's thoughts, emotions, and behaviors. The result is a therapy that focuses on inside to outside fixes, rather than only covering up the outside symptoms while ignoring the inside problems. You can feel confident in knowing that CBT makes a real and lasting change to a person as a whole, allowing them to continue to experience improvements even after the course of therapy has ended.

Myth #6: There is Limited Scientific Evidence Supporting CBT

The truth is that cognitive-behavioral therapy has a high degree of science-based evidence supporting its success, especially when compared to other forms of psychological therapies. A meta-analysis published by the University of Boston analyzed over one-hundred studies on the use of CBT for various disorders, addictions, sources of stress, and other possible circumstances. This meta-analysis revealed that in almost all cases, CBT was more effective than other forms of therapy used. Not only that, but it was found to be especially effective for individuals with anxiety disorders, general stress, anger control problems, bulimia, and somatoform disorders.

Myth #7: CBT Requires the Person to be Motivated

It can be hard to get started on therapy, even if you know it will help. When you are depressed or anxious it can be difficult to do anything, even what is best. Does this mean that CBT won't work for unmotivated people? No! In fact, most people are struggling with these issues when they begin and are, therefore, unmotivated. Yet, despite this lack of motivation, time and again these people find success and find themselves experiencing amazing benefits.

Even for a person lacking motivation, CBT works if they have a schedule with goals, preparation techniques, and a person to stay accountable to. By having someone on your side - even when you lack motivation - you have the aid of someone pushing you to stick to your schedule and continue using the techniques you have learned. This person is a therapist for most people; however, you can also stay accountable to a friend or a family member. The person who you are accountable to should understand the premise behind your therapy, so try to get them to read this book or show them highlights that will help them understand the process. If the person understands what you need to do, they can ensure you are doing it well and can give advice when needed.

Myth #8: It's Long/Short-Term Psychotherapy

People tend to believe that CBT is either long or short-term. The truth is somewhere in the middle. Unlike some forms of therapy that require a person to go multiple times a week for an unforeseeable amount of time, CBT has a set number of sessions. By the end of these sessions, the patient should find that they have restructured their cognition and are ready to go back out into the world on their own. They may still use the techniques they have learned to maintain healthy cognition, but they will no longer need to practice extensive therapy daily.

On the other hand, it is not necessarily a short-term therapy, either. While there are usually a set number of five to twenty weekly sessions, the number of sessions will go on as long as is needed for the individual. You don't have to worry about only getting five sessions if your case needs twenty.

Myth #9: CBT is Really Easy

It is true that cognitive-behavioral therapy is a simple and straightforward therapy that anyone can accomplish, adult or child. However, it is important to keep in mind that no therapy is "really easy." All forms of therapy will have their own struggles, as it is not easy to overcome our inner pain, trauma, or habits. Restructuring your cognition into a more balanced and healthier worldview will take diligence and hard work. You will have to ensure you use your learned techniques on a daily basis and remain honest with yourself.

At the end of your time using CBT, you will find that the effort and work you put into restructuring your cognition was well worth it. Sure, it might not always be the easiest thing, but it is one of the most worthwhile ways you can spend your time. With diligent daily effort, you can find yourself much more balanced, satisfied, and happy.

Common Mistakes

It is common to make mistakes occasionally with any form of therapy. Usually, your therapist will help to correct these mistakes and guide you along the right path. However, if you are using CBT alone and without the aid of a therapist, you will need to keep these common mistakes in mind so that you can avoid them.

Mistake #1: Not Understanding the Importance of Repetition

People who have tried cognitive therapy, either with a misunderstanding of the process or without a CBT-specialized therapist, may be frustrated and say that the process does not work, that it's a failure. However, studies show us repeatedly that when a therapist who specializes in CBT employs the process on their patients, the process is effective. So, why the difference in experiences? Simply put, if a person uses a therapist who does not understand the process or they try it on their own without the proper knowledge, they will make mistakes, and these mistakes don't promote progress.

One of the biggest mistakes that lead to failure is not understanding the importance of repetition. A person can be told how they should and shouldn't think, but that does not mean they will automatically change. Instead, they must use techniques and tools to promote this change in their daily life. Every day - and throughout the day - they must use these techniques. This is because the key to successful CBT is a repetition of helpful techniques and balanced thinking. It takes consistent work.

Unlike other forms of therapy, you don't simply talk to a therapist and then go along your way for the week. You must put in the effort to directly change your cognition, and you do this by repeatedly using the tools and knowledge given to you. In the same way that you can't master archery by shooting off a dozen arrows, you can't master restructuring your cognition by using a few techniques a single time. With both of these, you must practice the same thing repeatedly in order to see a change and eventually master the craft. You can't expect results without practice.

Mistake #2: Using Positive Thinking in Place of CBT

We mentioned previously that some people may believe that positive thinking is all that CBT entails, which couldn't be further from the truth. With cognitive behavioral therapy, a person is restructuring their cognition to act in a more balanced manner. On the other hand, too often positive thinking is either insincere or refuses to see the negativity that is plain as day. The truth is that while we don't want to think in a negative way, it is important that we can see problems and the negatives in our lives in order to fix and overcome them. Ignoring negativity is like refusing to see a tornado that is headed right your way. The opposite of this (refusing to see something positively), would be a person lying in the fetal position crying "We're going to die" and refusing to do anything about the storm barreling closer. With a balanced cognition, you should be able to acknowledge the tornado coming your way, but also do something about it and move into the storm shelter for safety.

Remember, CBT is not about positive or negative thinking, *it is about a balanced cognition.*

Mistake #3: Not Making Use of Relaxation Techniques

Frequently therapists will get reports back from their patients, explaining that they are feeling stressed and anxious. When asked if they are using the relaxation techniques they were given, such as deep breathing and mindfulness, the person may respond *"Not really"* or *"a few times."* The problem with this is that you can't expect to benefit from something that you aren't using frequently and actively. Think about it, while we all would love it if we could start to lose weight simply by eating healthy for one day, we have to practice eating healthfully regularly in order to see results. The same is true of relaxation techniques. If you want to benefit from these techniques, lowing stress and reducing anxiety then you will need to put in the effort frequently.

These techniques train the mind and body to deal with negative emotions in a calm and productive manner, making way for positive emotions. Not only are they only beneficial on the days you practice them, but they also become more powerful the more frequently you use them. Think of these techniques like exercises: you get better and stronger the longer and more often you practice. Before long, you will find it simple to complete mindfulness and deep breathing simultaneously, but at first, it could be difficult for you to focus and sit still for long periods.

Keep putting in the practice with these techniques at least once or twice a day and you will find your stress and anxiety decreasing greatly over the next few weeks. Just don't slack off once your stress does reduce, keep practicing these daily regardless, as they will keep your stress low.

Mistake #4: Believing Emotions are Irrational

Since our ideas and feelings are based on our cognition, some people begin to believe that their feelings must be completely irrational. That if they were being balanced and rational than they wouldn't feel anything at all. But the truth is that feelings can be rational, irrational, or neutral. After all, you can feel irrationally angry when someone makes an innocent mistake, or you can be rationally angry at injustice and senseless violence that has occurred.

Humans are emotional beings, and you can't simply write off all of our emotions. They are an important part of ourselves that allow us to process the world around us, connect with a community, and become more compassionate. You are not meant to be a robot without any emotion, you are much more than someone's and zeros making up code. Numbness and a lack of emotions is a trademark symptom of severe depression. Therefore, don't try to rid yourself of these emotions. You can see a more balanced cognition while still benefiting from these valuable feelings.

Mistake #5: Using CBT to Justify a Lack of Responsibility

With cognitive behavioral therapy, a person is taught to embrace who they are and appreciate all aspects of themselves. This is meant to be used as a foundation to grow and improve upon yourself. Yet, some people take this as an excuse to just feel good about themselves and not worry about growth. They might embrace their flaws to such an extent that they don't care if they hurt others with these flaws. You often see this in people who brag about speaking bluntly or honestly. Yes, it is a good thing to speak honestly, but often when people are bragging about it, they are only using "honesty" as a reason to say cruel and unnecessary things.

With CBT you must see all of your attributes, both the good and the bad. Be proud of yourself for the good attributes, forgive the bad, and then try to grow and lessen the more negative attributes about yourself. This is nothing to be discouraged by - we are all human and have our own negative attributes. Throughout life, these attributes will change, and it is simply our job to constantly be working on ourselves, improving ourselves to be the best version of ourselves we can be.

Mistake #6: Demanding Rationality

As you learn about the importance of rational and balanced cognition and the benefits it offers, you will want to begin to restructure your cognition. However, some people will take this to the extreme of chastising themselves for not matching up to an imaged standard, believing that they should always be completely rational.

The truth is that this is in itself not rational, as it is an unrealistic expectation that is impossible to achieve. Again, we are humans who make mistakes; therefore, we cannot be one-hundred percent rational at all times. This is not what CBT is about or teaches. Simply, the purpose of restructuring our cognition is to improve our mental health and stress by viewing the world and ourselves more realistically.

This is also an irrational thought as it is black-or-white thinking that says, "If something isn't good, then it must be bad." With this therapy, you aren't meant to see everything in black and white, but instead, see that there are a variety of shades of these two colors in between.

Mistake #7: Not Making a Lifestyle Change

With cognitive behavioral therapy, you are not simply learning to recognize irrational or negative thinking to avoid. Instead, you are actively training your cognition to respond differently to stimulus. You are unable to train your brain if you do not put in the practice hours; simply reading this book will not do the trick! Yes, reading this book is the first step, but it won't help you if you don't put it into practice daily.

Think about it, you can't just run a marathon by reading a book about how to run more effectively. Instead, you have to get up every day and train for months at a time. The same is true of cognitive-behavioral therapy. For a few months, you will have to put in regular daily practice if you hope to truly make a change and succeed. If you want to restructure your cognition, you can't do it by reading a few words on a page. You must actively use the techniques and tools you have learned every day, all day.

It may take time, but if you make a lifestyle change by fully adopting CBT into your daily routine, you will soon find yourself improving. After a few weeks, you will notice a big improvement, and in a few months, the difference will be drastic.

Chapter 4: An In-Depth Look into What CBT Can Treat and Why it Works

Cognitive-behavioral therapy has been used for decades to treat depression and anxiety disorders, but there are many other conditions it can be used to treat, as well. For instance, it can be used in the treatment of bipolar disorders, phobias, obsessive-compulsive disorder, post-traumatic stress disorder, eating disorders, substance addictions, and more. In this chapter, you will get an in-depth look at some of the more common conditions that CBT is best used for.

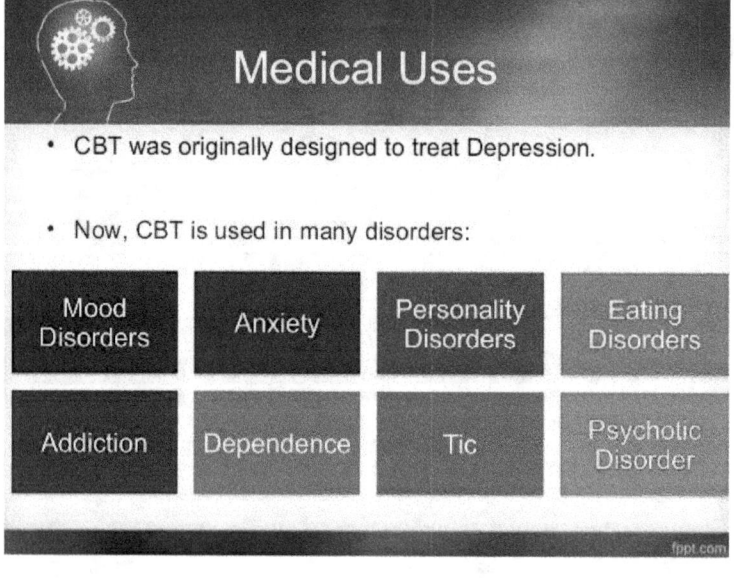

[Medical uses of CBT. Originally created to treat depression, now CBT is used in many disorders. Examples include mood disorders, anxiety, personality disorders, eating disorders, addiction, dependence, tics, and psychotic disorders.]

Depression

Depression, otherwise known as major depressive disorder, is a truly devastating condition. Many people can go a long time without a diagnosis because they aren't aware that what they are feeling *isn't what everyone else feels*. They may also be afraid to speak up and share their experience with family, friends, or their doctor. This is incredibly dangerous, as the longer depression goes untreated, the worse it can get, and it may lead to suicidal thoughts or attempts. Even if the person never attempts suicide, they will live feeling miserable and may attempt to harm themselves in other ways. Nobody deserves to live this way; it is truly terrible. Please, if you suspect you may have depression talk to your doctor. Some symptoms include:

- Feelings of worthlessness, guilt, emptiness, or hopelessness
- An emotional numb feeling
- Loss of interest in activities
- Out-of-body experiences
- Irritability in adolescents and children
- Thoughts of death, injury, or self-harm
- Feeling fatigued and low energy
- A desire to sleep, even when not tired
- Difficulty making decisions
- Poor concentration
- Insomnia or hypersomnia

- Weight loss or gain

Sadly, depression affects a large number of the population. This can affect people differently, with some people only experiencing occasional short bouts of depression, others experiencing seasonal depression, and worse: those who suffer from long-term major depression. The lifetime depression prevalence rate in America is seventeen percent, with about seven percent of the population suffering from this disorder rarely. While men also develop depression, women are two to three times more likely to develop this disorder. People who have other physical or mental illnesses are also at a higher risk of developing depression.

For short-term depression, medication often lacks effectiveness, but medication is an important part of the treatment in long-term depression. With long-term depression, most people need a combination of both medicine and therapy, whereas people with short-term depression are often most helped with therapy. Make sure you talk to your doctor about your treatment options, as depression is not something you want to take lightly.

Cognitive-behavioral therapy has been proven to be an effective treatment option, often in conjunction with antidepressants, for people with both short-term and long-term depression. When a person begins CBT with a therapist for depression, the therapy sessions will begin with the therapist first explaining the CBT process to the patient and how it is ideal for depression. Then, the patient and therapist will work together to set treatment goals, learn behavioral skills, and techniques to use daily. When a person is using CBT specifically for depression the focus of treatment will be on helping the patient become involved in more activities that are important to them - yet hard to accomplish due to the depression. Learning to better interact with the world and be kind to themselves are other aspects the therapist and patient will focus on.

People with depression regularly experience negative thoughts and beliefs about themselves, the world, the future, and other people.

This is one reason why CBT is so powerful in treating depression. Many of the techniques and tools of CBT are created specifically to help a person analyze these negative thoughts and balance them into something more truthful and positive. Over time, this restructures the cognition so that the depressed person no longer thinks as negatively or catastrophically. As their cognition becomes balanced and they think less negatively, the person will experience fewer symptoms of depression and be able to better enjoy life again. This process can even be altered for children and intellectually disabled people so that parents or caregivers can help them use the techniques if they are unable to do it alone.

In short, CBT works for depression because it helps people enjoy activities again and think less negatively, which are the trademark symptoms of this disorder.

If you choose to see a professional CBT-trained therapist for your treatment, you can expect to have one therapy session a week for ten to twenty weeks. Each of these sessions will likely follow a set order, which includes a check on the patient's mood, bridging the previous and current therapy sessions together, review of the previous week's homework, setting an agenda for the following week, discussing the agenda, homework assignments, and a summary of the session. During these sessions, the patient can ask any questions or discuss any problems that occur so that the therapist can walk them through a solution.

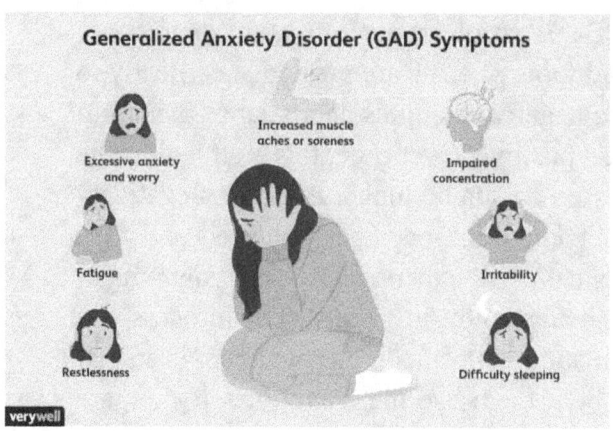

[Generalized Anxiety Disorder (GAD) Symptoms: restlessness, fatigue, excessive anxiety and worry, increased muscle aches or soreness, impaired concentration, irritability, and difficulty sleeping.]

General Anxiety Disorder and Social Anxiety Disorder

There are many types of anxiety disorders, such as generalized anxiety disorder, social anxiety disorder, panic disorder, obsessive-compulsive disorder, and more. However, while all types of anxiety disorders we treated well with CBT, they require different techniques and methods. Therefore, we will be discussing these disorders separately. In this section, we will be examining how cognitive behavioral therapy can help those with generalized anxiety disorder and social anxiety disorder.

Anxiety attacks can cause relentless worry, panic attacks, and incapacitating fear, but you don't have to live this way. Treatment is possible, and there is a long track record of CBT being the best option for those suffering from anxiety disorders. While some people may require medication, this therapy works because it does not simply cover up the problems, but instead, it treats the main problem that causes anxiety. You can learn how to overcome the fears and unease that cause the anxiety, how to better relax, look at life in a more balanced approach, create coping mechanisms, and learn problem-solving skills. You are not only learning tools that can help your anxiety, but you are also taught how to use them for a better life.

Generalized Anxiety Disorder, otherwise known as GAD, is the most common form of anxiety disorder that people experience. GAD is characterized by excessive and persistent worry and fear. This fear can be about oneself, others, the world, the future, or practically anything else. Oftentimes, people worry about family, work, money, health, and other pressing issues in life. However, unlike most individuals, those with GAS are unable to control or manage their worry and fear on their own, leading it to become a nightmare. They may become to expect the worst, even when there is no apparent reason for worry. Often, people develop insomnia (an inability to sleep) as their worries worsen when they lay down for the night without distractions.

Women are twice as likely to develop GAD as men, and three percent of the population (nearly seven million adults) are diagnosed with a generalized anxiety disorder. How is it diagnosed? Your doctor can diagnose the condition if you find you worry more days than not for a period of at least six months.

People with GAD may experience anxiety about specific events such as work, people such as family, or it may simply be overwhelming anxiety without any known cause. A person may feel a rush of anxiety about nothing more than getting through the day or getting out of bed. There does not have to be a specific thing causing the worry, the anxiety is there regardless. Not only does this cause overwhelming worry, but this constant anxiety can also trigger stomachaches, fatigue, and headaches.

Many people with mild or moderate GAD, or those receiving treatment, are able to live normally within society. They are able to hold a decent job, enjoy their social life, and live the meaningful life they desire. However, many people with uncontrolled GAD may avoid social situations, travel, employment promotions, or other simple daily activities. Yet, there is hope for these people. With the treatment in the form of CBT, they can once again live the life they desire.

[Social Anxiety Disorder Risk Factors: genetics, observing others with SAD, early traumatic events, parenting styles, isolated upbringing, brain structure, and social expectations.]

Social anxiety is similar to generalized anxiety disorder, but it has a more specific cause. With SAD a person is specifically anxious about interacting with other people. It is an intense worry of being rejected and judged by their peers. This can result in the person with SAD acting visibly anxious by stumbling overworks, acting awkward, and blushing, which may even result in the being viewed by others as weird, boring, or "stupid." Sadly, this only causes the social anxiety to worsen, as in their minds the anxiety they were feeling was proven to be true.

Often, people with SAD experience physical symptoms as well, such as sweating, nausea, increased heart rate, and sometimes they may even experience full-blown anxiety or panic attacks when confronted with a situation they fear such as public speaking. A person with

SAD may recognize that their fear is excessive or unreasonable, but they also feel powerless to stop the anxiety.

There are approximately fifteen-million Americans living with social anxiety disorder, making it the second most common type of anxiety disorder after phobias. SAD will frequently develop during the teenage years, continuing to affect the person into adulthood. People with this condition may have been excessively shy during childhood, but it is important to note that there is a big difference between basic shyness and social anxiety disorder.

Social anxiety frequently disrupts the life of the individual with the condition. They may avoid job opportunities that require interactions with more people, reduce the number of social interactions, avoid stores with crowds, and may even isolate themselves from their friends. It can be really hard for a person with SAD to succeed in work or school without treatment. Unfortunately, fewer than five percent of the people with SAD seek treatment within a year of onset, and a third of the people with this condition experience symptoms for more than ten years before seeking help.

Cognitive-behavioral therapy is often the best treatment course for both generalized anxiety disorder and social anxiety disorder. The tools that promote rationality, repetition, and reinforcement have been proven to be more effective in treatment than other methods.

Some of the benefits for those with anxiety disorder follow, below.

- **Learning to Tolerate Uncertainty**

One of the key factors in these two anxiety disorders is uncertainty. If a person with an anxiety disorder isn't one-hundred percent sure that a negative event won't take place they feel agitated and uncertain, increasing their anxiety.

This intolerance to uncertainty not only increases anxiety, but it can delay decision making, increase procrastination, lead to a refusal to delegate, and causes excessive checking.

CBT helps a person learn to cope with uncertainty, thereby eliminating this source of anxiety and making them more productive in their day-to-day life.

- **Recognize Rumination**

Rumination is the process of continuously worrying about the same subject. For instance, a person may constantly worry about if they are going to get a job promotion for an entire week or two. This causes a reduction in problem-solving capabilities and increases general worry. Instead of ruminating on a problem, it is best to wait and deal with problem-solving the situation when it occurs.

There are several CBT techniques that are used to help decrease rumination, such as mindfulness and diffusion techniques. You will learn to accept whatever thoughts you are having, recognize that they might not be completely accurate, and then allowing them to pass by. With CBT, you don't try to block these thoughts, as that is ineffective. When you instead acknowledge your thoughts and then let them go, you are better able to release the anxiety.

- **Recognize Thought Distortions**

We all have thought distortions to an extent, but people with SAD and GAD tend to have them in a higher number and to a worse degree. Thought distortions can take many forms, such as underestimating our own abilities, negatively predicting the future, personalizing negative experiences, black and white judgments, catastrophically circumstances, negatively predicting what others might possibly think, entitlements, and more.

With CBT, a person is learning to recognize these distortions and then replace them with more balanced thoughts. This allows the person to slowly restructure their cognition until they experience these distortions less frequently.

- **Adopt Mindfulness Techniques**

CBT frequently uses mindfulness, deep breathing, and muscle relaxation. These techniques help a person reduce their avoidance mechanisms and instead work on improving their anxiety head-on. Instead of continuing to wade into a pool of fear, worry, and rumination a person is taught to directly deal with and lessen anxiety. This can easily be done in five to ten-minute sessions whenever a person is feeling anxious.

- **Treat Yourself Kindly**

It is all too common for people with anxiety disorders to speak harshly to themselves, noting their imperfections and doubting their abilities. When this happens, it often leads to rumination and avoidance mechanisms. However, studies have shown that by increasing self-kindness we can also decrease anxiety and increase self-improvement motivation. Cognitive-behavioral therapy uses many different techniques and tools to promote self-kindness and forgiveness, thereby decreasing a person's anxiety and increasing their motivation.

It is important to remember that while CBT is often the best treatment option for anxiety disorders, there is no quick fix. While you will see improvement in a number of weeks, it will take several months until you see the full benefit that cognitive-behavioral therapy has to offer. Don't give up after a single day or a week, you need to consistently put in the effort if you hope to see the results of your labor. Sometimes people may even feel worse before they feel better, as they are facing their anxieties and overcoming them rather than ignoring them as they have in the past. However, if you follow your therapist's advice or the knowledge you gain from this book - and continue to put in the effort - you will not lose.

Along with the techniques for cognitive behavioral therapy, it is also wise to adopt other healthy lifestyle practices. By cultivating a healthier life, you will be supporting your CBT and enabling yourself to improve more quickly and successfully.

Some healthy lifestyle factors you should consider adding into your daily life include learning about your anxiety disorder, deepening connections with other people, reducing anxiety stressors, and cultivating a healthy body.

When learning about anxiety you can better understand how your mind works, allowing you to better defeat the negative thoughts that come your way. By deepening your connections with other people, you can decrease loneliness and isolation. You will have more support and feel at ease to have a trusted loved one. Reducing stressors such as toxic relationships and unneeded pressure will decrease unnecessary worry, allowing you to have more energy for what is important in your life. Lastly, by creating a healthy mind by eating well, exercising, and avoiding drugs you can strengthen and improve your mind.

Post-Traumatic Stress Disorder

People often think about this anxiety disorder as only something military members who have been deployed to war zones experience, but this is not true. Anyone can develop post-traumatic stress disorder, or PTSD, if they have undergone a traumatic event. Terrorist attacks, serious accidents, natural disasters, sexual assault, violent attacks, and more can all cause a person to develop PTSD.

The misunderstanding of PTSD - and the belief that it only affects the military - is due to it originally being named "shell shock" to describe veterans with PTSD after World War I. Thankfully, while laypeople still have misunderstandings of PTSD, the medical community recognizes that it can happen to anyone. Approximately 3.5 percent of Americans suffer from this form of anxiety.

What, exactly, is it like to experience PTSD? People with this condition experience disturbing, scary, and anxiety-inducing thoughts, feelings, and memories long after a traumatic experience has ended. For instance, a person who was attacked by a dog may, later on, continue to think about the attack, having anxiety and panic attacks whenever they hear a dog bark or think they see a dog. A person does not even have to experience the traumatic event themselves to develop PTSD, they can develop it simply by hearing second-hand about a traumatic event.

There are specific criteria a doctor will use to diagnose a person with PTSD. However, some of the most common symptoms and effects include:

• Inability to remember aspects of the traumatic events (not caused by drugs, alcohol, or head injury).

• Distorted blame of oneself or others.

• Negative and exaggerated beliefs or expectations about the world, others, or oneself.

• Aggressive or irritable behavior.

• Feelings of detachment from others.

• Persistent shame, guilt, fear, anger, or horror.

• Self-destructive or reckless behavior.

• Inability to feel positive emotions.

• Diminished interest in activities.

• Hypervigilance.

• Difficulty concentrating.

• More easily startled.

• Emotional numbness and avoidance of reminders of the trauma.

• Distressing flashbacks or nightmares about the traumatic event.

• Trouble falling or staying asleep.

• More easily jumpy, angry, or irritated.

• Panic attacks (heart palpitations, tachycardia, dizziness, trouble breathing).

There are various theories as to why people develop PTSD, one of these is the social cognitive theory by Benight and Bandura. This theory explains that people who have experienced trauma attempt to process the event into beliefs about the world, others, and oneself. However, when they are processing these thoughts and emotions a person might end up creating harmful misunderstandings about their experience, the world, others, themselves, and their perception of control. For example, a person may believe that bad things happen to bad people, therefore having experienced a traumatic event they may feel that they are bad, and it was their "punishment."

A person with PTSD is encouraged to isolate these misconceptions and distortions they have created, in order to process the trauma. These distortions are then reevaluated and turned into a more balanced and truthful thinking pattern. It takes time, but if a person regularly journals and categorizes their harmful thoughts into balanced thoughts, they will begin to have a less distorted cognition, finding that the PTSD slowly improving.

A therapist may also guide the patient through controlled exposure therapy to help lessen flashbacks, nightmares, and panic attacks when confronted with reminders to the traumatic event. This is done slowly and carefully, often starting with the patient closing their eyes and thinking about safely interacting with a trigger. For instance, if the person was attacked by a dog, they might safely interact with a small well-behaved dog. If this is too much, they can imagine that the dog is inside a kennel and unable to get close to them. Once the person is able to handle thinking about interacting with triggers, they will likely move onto actually interacting with the triggers in life. The therapist will allow the person to see a well-behaved dog on a leash at a distance and continue to progress until the person is finally able to stand next to - or pet - a dog. How exposure therapy works greatly varies, depending on the type of trauma a person experienced, but a well-trained therapist should be able to walk their patient through the process.

Obsessive-Compulsive Disorder

Commonly known as OCD, obsessive-compulsive disorder is a type of anxiety disorder that results in frequent, unwanted, recurring thoughts, sensations, or ideas. These recurrent thoughts often make people act on them compulsively, resulting in them being known as "compulsions." This can include repetitive behaviors such as checking on things, hand washing, cleaning, keeping objects in order or symmetrical, and more. It may also include unwanted thoughts, such as those that are aggressive or sexual in nature.

There are many people without OCD who experienced repetitive behaviors or focused thought. Yet, these don't interfere with their daily lives, they may even make life easier for the person. However, for people with OCD, these repeated behaviors and unwanted thoughts cause the person unimaginable stress if they are *unable to act on them*. For instance, a person with OCD may wash their hands to the point that the skin is raw and coming off, yet they are unable to stop. Another person suffering from OCD may be unable to leave the house if they don't first check the stove ten times and turn the doorknob from left to right in a specific pattern perfectly three times.

People with OCD may logically know that nothing disastrous will happen if they don't act on these repetitive behaviors and thoughts, but even with logically understanding this, their obsessions remain. They have a difficult time not focusing on repetitive thoughts or acting on the compulsive actions. It can become so severe that if the person is unable to act on the compulsion, they experience a panic attack and may even harm themselves.

Many people have misunderstandings of what OCD is and think it's a joke, repeating harmful stereotype jokes such as "I love cleaning, I must be OCD!" or "I have OCD, Obsessive Christmas Disorder." Yet, despite these misunderstandings, the truth is that only a small percent of the population actually has OCD, with the statistics showing over just over one percent.

With cognitive behavioral therapy, a person can learn to cope and change their problematic thoughts, emotions, and behaviors, thereby treating the source of the OCD. When a person has OCD, their therapist will use a particular subset of CBT known as exposure and ritual prevention. The purpose of this type of CBT is to restructure the cognition and break the previously ingrained associations. There are two ways this can help. First, it will break the feelings of distress from the triggers that produce this feeling, such as thoughts, situations, or objects. Second, it will break the connection between acting on ritualistic behaviors and the experience of decreased stress. This means that over time, a person's stress will decrease overall and their brain will no longer believe that they need to act on the repetitive thoughts or behaviors.

Three steps to CBT treatment for the obsessive-compulsive disorder include:

- **Imagined Exposure**

With imagined exposure, a person mentally visualizes themselves in a situation that is usually distressing - or the consequences of a feared situation. For instance, they might imagine starting a kitchen fire and having to deal with the results.

- **Real-Life Exposure**

With this step, a person will expose themselves to a feared situation or object that triggers anxiety. This might be germs, a messy space, or any other trigger.

- **Ritual Prevention**

In this step, a person avoids acting on ritualistic behaviors. This means that they might leave the kitchen without checking on the stove or touch a dog without washing their hands afterward.

Addiction

There are many addictions, but two of the most common and problematic are drug and alcohol related. No matter the addiction, depression, and anxiety are often the root cause, which is one reason why CBT is well-known to help.

People who frequently experience negative thinking have difficulty making changes, even those that they know are best for them. This means that even if a person wants to give up alcohol, drugs, or other addictions, they may have a difficult time making the changes needed to break the addiction. These are powerful and destructive thoughts and may frequently occur as all-or-nothing thinking. This type of thinking makes people believe they lack control and are powerless over their behavior regarding their addiction. For instance, they may believe that they have to do everything perfectly because anything less is a failure. This type of thinking often results in a reliance on drugs, alcohol, gambling, or even video games.

When an addict begins treatment with CBT, they will learn to dismantle the false ideas and insecurities that lead to their substance abuse, be provided with tools and self-help guides to improve their moods, learn better communication skills, and be given tools to use when they feel compelled to act on their addiction.

As you can see, cognitive behavioral therapy can help people with many different disorders. Whether you are struggling with a generalized anxiety disorder or drug addiction, you can find help with CBT. There are many other psychological conditions that this therapy can help as well, so don't feel discouraged if your problem wasn't described in detail here.

Chapter 5: The Key Principles of Cognitive Behavioral Therapy

In this chapter, we will focus on the key principles of CBT, such as why the human brain operates certain ways, how CBT techniques affect the human cognition, and how you can go about restructuring your cognition. This chapter contains an in-depth look at the key factors of cognitive-behavioral therapy.

The goal of CBT is to teach individuals how to recognize their distorted ideas through an evaluation process of negative or anxiety-inducing thoughts. Once people learn to recognize these thoughts, they can then learn to tell truth from fiction and how to replace the false ideas with those that are more balanced and truthful. Over time, the individual will learn how to observe and monitor their thoughts regularly, allowing them to catch harmful thoughts and patterns before they become ingrained in their cognition.

Homework is an important part of CBT. Whether you are doing the therapy with the aid of a therapist or on your own, it is vital that you use the techniques and tools that are common with this therapy process. If you don't use these methods on a daily basis you will be unable to improve. After all, you will never learn to run a marathon if you don't exercise, and you won't be able to gain a healthy cognition if you don't complete your therapy homework.

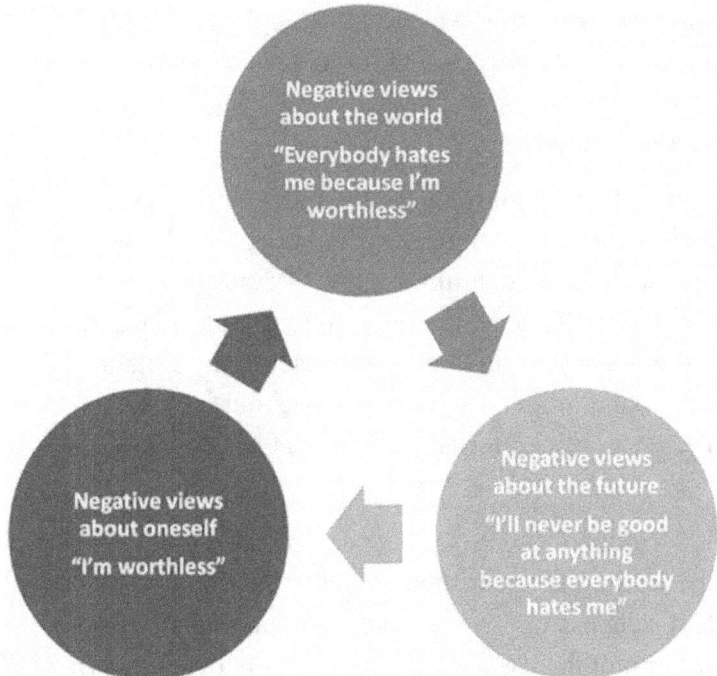

[Model of the cognitive triad. A triangle shape with three points leading to each other. Going clockwise these points are negative views about the world, such as "Everybody hates me because I'm worthless"; negative views about the future, such as "I'll never be good at anything because everybody hates me"; and negative views about oneself, such as "I'm worthless."]

There are a few theories of CBT that are important to keep in mind, as these will help you to better understand the therapy process, increasing your success:

1. It is believed that abnormality in the human brain is a result of cognitive distortions regarding us, others, the future, or the world as a whole.

2. These cognitive distortions are likely caused by irrational thought and cognitive triad. The negative tried includes negative views of the world, negative views of the future, and negative views of oneself.

3. The way we interact with the world is through our mental representation of the world. This means that if we have an inaccurate representation or if our reasoning is inefficient then our emotions and behavior can become distorted.

Dr. Albert Ellis believed that we all hold our own set of assumptions about the world and ourselves, and these assumptions serve as a guide throughout life to help us determine how to react to various situations and circumstances. Sadly, these assumptions are largely affected by irrational thought, causing people to react to the situation in inappropriate ways that might, in turn, reduce our chance of success and happiness. Dr. Ellis referred to these as "basic irrational assumptions."

Some of us develop irrational thoughts that we are failures or that others don't love us, leading to a constant search for validation and approval, only to feel rejected in the end. Every interaction a person has is affected by this irrational assumption, meaning that even if we have a great time with friends we can, later on, feel dissatisfied doubting that those we interacted with truly enjoy spending time with us. You may feel that people are only being kind and acting as if they are friends with you when really, they think you're "weird" or "stupid."

Dr. Ellis listed several types of basic irrational assumptions, which include:

- The idea that past history greatly influences your present
- The idea that a person should be perfect at everything
- The idea that people don't have control over their own happiness
- The idea that you need a stronger person to depend on
- The idea that things are catastrophic when they don't go your way

- The idea that there is a perfect solution to your problems, and it's disastrous if you don't find it

Dr. Ellis believed that people regularly hold onto these basic irrational assumptions with force, as they are a part of their cognition. Therefore, a therapist must use vigorous techniques of cognitive-behavioral therapy in order to get their patients to change their irrational thinking. Often times, the ABC Technique of Irrational Beliefs is used for this process.

Let's have a look at this technique. Keep in mind that there are three columns: A, B, and C.

A – Activating Event or Objective Situation:	B – Beliefs:	C – Consequences:
In the A column, a person records an objective situation. This is a situation that leads to negative dysfunctional thinking or high emotional response.	In the B column, a person writes down whatever negative ideas or thoughts occurred to them.	In the third column, column C, a person details what dysfunctional behavioral or negative feelings A and B resulted in.

While a difficult situation will be obviously difficult no matter our interpretation of the event, how these events affect us emotionally and our reactions depend on our beliefs. Dr. Ellis believed that it wasn't column A, the activating event that causes our negative feelings, but rather column B with our beliefs about the event that results in the negative feelings from column C.

For instance, a person may be upset after getting a bad score on a test. The activating event (A) is that the person failed the test. The belief (B) is that they are worthless if they don't get high grades. The consequence (C), is that the person now feels depressed.

After a person works through finding their irrational beliefs, they can then work on challenging the narrative and reframing it in a more realistic and balanced light. This helps a person to develop a more rational cognition and healthy coping mechanisms, which only improve overtime as they continue to reframe their cognition.

If this person was seeing a therapist, the therapist would walk them through the process, explaining that there is no evidence that a person is only worthwhile if they achieve high grades or that getting low grades. While the person may desire high grades and it is a good thing to have, the absence of this does not cause a person to be worthless.

This is helpful because the person can learn that while it is disappointing to get a bad grade or to not be good at studying, they are still not a bad person. They will feel frustration, but not depressed and worthless. In fact, this type of frustration can be a source of healthy motivation to encourage the person to study better in the future, increasing their chances of future success.

Like the previously mentioned example, there are many types of cognitive distortions. These distortions reinforce inaccurate and negative thought patterns, behaviors, and emotions. It is important to be fully aware of the different type of distortions, as you cannot recognize and restructure your distortions if you don't first understand what is and isn't a distortion. Let's have a look at the fifteen identified distortions.

1. Filtering

With filtering, a person will ignore all of the good and positive circumstances in their life to instead focus only on the negative. This is a trap of negativity that causes a person to dwell in anything bad while ignoring the abundance of good surrounding them.

2. Black and White Thinking

With black and white thinking, there is no room for nuance or complexity. A person views everything without any shades of gray, in only black or white. This means that if you don't perform perfectly in every area, then you will see yourself as a complete failure, rather than recognizing that you are a complex person that may be unskilled in some areas - while excelling in others.

3. Overgeneralization

When a person overgeneralizes, they use a sole incident or a single piece of evidence and use it to reach a broad conclusion. For example, a person may fail to get into the college of their choice, and instead of brushing off the situation as a single bad experience and trying again at another college, they decide that they are not fit for college and will never get accepted.

4. Conclusion Jumping

This distortion is similar to overgeneralization. With conclusion jumping, a person has a distortion that leads to faulty reasoning in how they make conclusions. However, unlike overgeneralization - which is the result of a single incident – with conclusion jumping, a person will jump to conclusions, assuming something without any evidence supporting it. For instance, a person might be convinced that their coworkers hate them, even without any real evidence.

5. Catastrophizing

With catastrophizing, a person believes that the worst will (or *already has*) happened, based on an incident that is nowhere near as extreme or catastrophic as they have made it out to be. For instance, someone might make a small mistake on some paperwork for their job, and therefore believe that their boss will go into a fury and fire them. In the same way, the person might minimize anything positive, such as their successes or desirable characteristics.

6. Personalization

With this distortion, a person comes to believe that everything they do has an external impact on people and events, no matter how unlikely or irrational it is. This person may feel that they are the cause of all bad things that occur around them. For example, they may believe that because they were a few minutes late to a meeting, the entire meeting went poorly, and that it would have gone better if they had just been on time or weren't there to begin with.

7. Control Fallacies

With this distortion, a person believes that everything that happens to them is either entirely due to their own actions or purely external forces. While it is true that at times situations occur due to our own actions - or sometimes due to outside forces - distortion takes place when a person assumes that a situation is always either one way or the other. For instance, a person may believe that their coworker's poor efforts are the cause for their own mistakes on the job, or they might believe that those around them are only making mistakes because of something they did. The truth is that situations occur due to a mix of our own actions and outside forces, not either-or/all or nothing.

8. Fairness Fallacy

Some people may focus on fairness to an extreme, creating a distortion. We all know that life isn't always fair, it's an often-sad reality. Because of this, if a person goes through life looking for it to be fair, they will experience disappointment and grow resentful. This is because life will sometimes go how we want and other times it won't, regardless of how far it appears.

9. The Blame Game

If something does not go our way, there are many ways in which we might assign responsibility or explain the outcome. One way that people do this is by blaming those around them whenever something goes wrong. For instance, if we feel angry or sad, we might blame others for making us feel that way. Yet, this is another cognitive distortion, as only we are responsible for our emotions and actions, nobody else is to blame.

10. Should Have

"Should have" refers to how we believe that we - and others - should behave. When people break our rules for how we believe they should behave, we become upset. If we break our own rules, then we feel guilty. For instance, you may have a rule that people should greet those they know when seeing each other. If a person does not greet you upon seeing you, you might feel angry and brushed off. By the same token, if you have a rule that you should save money, you might feel guilty if you buy yourself a coffee, even if it was only a small amount of money.

11. Emotional Reasoning

With emotional reasoning, a person believes that if they think a certain way, then it must be true. For instance, they may FEEL ugly, boring, or awkward at the moment, therefore they believe that they are truly ugly, boring and awkward. Simply put, they believe that if they feel something, it is automatically true. However, if we have a balanced cognition then we should be able to recognize that our emotions do not always indicate what the objective truth of a situation is.

12. Change Fallacy

With this fallacy, we believe other people should change as we see fit. This also attaches to the belief that our happiness relies on other people, and that if these people are unable or unwilling to change, then they are preventing us from attaining happiness. This distortion is harmful for two reasons. First, because it makes us believe that we are not responsible for our own happiness that it is in the control of other people. Second, because it leads us to try and take control over the lives of others.

13. Mislabeling

Mislabeling is similar to overgeneralization, but it is taken to an extreme. With mislabeling we take one or two instances and generalize them into a judgment on a global scale. For instance, if we fail at a single task, we may believe that we are a total failure, not only in that area - but in all areas. On another hand, if someone is rude to us, we may believe that they, as an entire person, are rude.

Mislabeling often uses loaded language, such as saying someone has "failed" their baby for using formula or disposable diapers rather than the alternatives.

14. Always Right

Everyone wants to be right, but, with this distortion, a person believes they must always be right, and that being wrong is completely unacceptable. A person with this distortion may believe that their being right is of greater importance than the feelings of others. This prevents them from being willing to admit when they made a mistake.

15. Heaven's Reward Fallacy

This last distortion involves a person expecting that they will be rewarded for self-denial or sacrifice. They may call it karma - or by another name – believing that this will always reward them for their good deeds. This can result in bitterness when a person does not receive a reward.

Thought Journaling

In order to deal with these dysfunctional thoughts and beliefs, a person should keep a dysfunctional thought record. This record will use the ABC Technique, mentioned earlier, to discover dysfunctional thoughts and to reframe them into something more balanced. However, unlike the ABC method, the thought journal is organized into seven columns instead of three. For instance:

1. On the far left of the page write out the first column. This will have the time and date that a dysfunctional thought occurred.

2. The next column is where you write out the situation that occurred leading up to when you experienced the dysfunctional thought. You will need to go into as much detail as possible here.

3. In the third column, you will write out the automatic dysfunctional thought you had, along with how much you believe this thought, from a scale of zero percent to one hundred percent.

4. In the fourth column, you will describe the emotions that were elicited by the dysfunctional thought, along with a scale of how strongly you experienced the various emotions from zero percent to one hundred percent.

5. In the fifth column, you will try to identify what type of distortion your thought belongs to. You will need to use the list of fifteen distortions in order to identify yours. Is it Change Fallacy? The Blame Game? Filtering? Go through the list and write down which most fits your distortion. This is important, as it will help you detect patterns and find which distortions you are most prone to.

6. In the next-to-last column, you will replace the distortion with a more balanced and healthy alternative thought.

7. In the final column, you will detail the outcome of the exercise. Through filling out this journal were you able to confront your dysfunctional thought? Were you able to create a more balanced thought? Did your negative emotions or thoughts decrease?

Fact-Checking

Another exercise that you might use is fact-checking. As we have a habit of believing that our thoughts are true, this exercise helps us determine whether or not our fears are backed by fact. For instance, you may have failed a test. This is a fact. However, that does not mean it is a fact that you are "dumb." These are non-factual opinions, not facts you should take to heart. However, because of our dysfunctional thoughts, it is hard to truly believe that these opinions aren't facts. Whenever you are struggling with dysfunctional thoughts or intense emotions try filling out this fact checklist.

To create this fact checklist simply write out three columns. In the first column, you will write the statements that we will list in a moment. The second column will be for adding a checkmark for all the statements that are true. The final column will be for adding a checkmark to any statements that are false. When filling out this list you simply check-in either the true or false column as you read down the list.

Now, let's get to the statements you will add to the first column:

- I'm a bad person
- I'm selfish
- I'm dumb
- I failed the test/exam
- Nobody likes me
- I'm m unattractive
- I will fail this test
- I have no friends
- I'm single
- My family is disappointed in me
- I'm overweight
- I will be single forever
- I didn't lend my friend money when asked
- I'm not good enough
- This will be a disaster
- I'm not good at my job
- I dislike my job

These are not trick questions, there will be a correct true or false answer to each of these statements. The purpose of these questions and fact-checking it to help your brain recognize fact from fiction. Since we all struggle with cognitive distortions that make us believe thoughts that are not true, it helps us to become better able to discern the difference between what is true and what isn't.

Cognitive Questioning

The method of cognitive questioning is a combination of thought journaling and fact-checking that uses Socratic questioning to allow us to determine whether or not our thoughts are rational or irrational.

To practice cognitive questioning, divide a piece of paper or page in a journal into three sections. The first section is titled "My Thought." This is where you can write down single or multiple thoughts that you suspect might be irrational, destructive, or negative.

In the middle section, you should write down any facts that either support or contradict the thoughts you are examining. What facts call into question your thought? What facts support the thought? Once you have gathered as much evidence as possible you can make a judgment on whether or not the thought was based on fact or opinion. The detail which thoughts are based on fact with a checkmark placed next to them in the first section, or with an x to mark which thoughts are based only on opinion.

In the last section on the page, you will go into Socratic questioning. The purpose of this is to further question the thoughts. Use the following questions to further analyze the thoughts:

- **Is this truly a black-and-white situation or are there shades of gray?**

You want to examine whether or not you are using all-or-nothing thinking, and if that is making the situation seem unreasonable complex or simple.

- **Am I making assumptions or misinterpreting evidence?**

It is easy to make assumptions or misinterpret evidence, even when we don't realize that we are doing so. Take some time to figure out if you are doing this.

- **Might other people interpret the situation differently? How might they interpret it?**

Think about someone close to you, such as a family member, friend, or coworker. How might they interpret the same situation?

- **Am I looking at all the evidence or only the evidence that supports what I already believe?**

- We may think we are being objective, but often people only want to consider evidence that supports what they already believe. Be sure that you aren't ignoring any evidence to the contrary.

- **Are these thoughts an over-inflation of the truth?**

Sometimes we have negative thoughts - not about the full truth - but about a partial truth that we have inflated past its logical boundaries.

- **Are these thoughts habitual?**

Cognitive distortions become a matter of habit over time, meaning that sometimes we are focused on thought not because facts truly support it, but only because it is a habit.

- **How did this thought first occur? Did someone else pass this thought on? Is this person trustworthy?**

Sometimes we only have thoughts because someone passed them onto us. For instance, we might start thinking negatively about our body after someone criticizes us.

Keeping the previous questions in mind, how likely is the original thought?

If you have irrational thoughts that plague you, then filling out this cognitive questioning list can help you to evaluate them for truth. This can help you not only identify the thoughts, but also diffuse them. When a thought is proven to be false, you will find that by seeing the answers plain as day, you will feel better.

Chapter 6: Overcoming Anxiety and Depression Step-By-Step

In this chapter, you will discover step-by-step how to overcome depression and anxiety with cognitive behavioral therapy. You will find that this chapter is sorted into weeks, with each week having its own homework. It is structured as if you were seeing a therapist weekly. However, to truly gain success, it is important that you stick to it. Don't skip your homework. EVER. You will only experience the benefits if you put in the work, but it will be well worth it.

Week One

The term "cognitive-behavioral therapy" has meaning. The word "cognitive" refers to our thoughts and "behavioral" refers to our actions. This is important to understand because our thoughts and actions affect our feelings, thereby either worsening or improving our mental health.

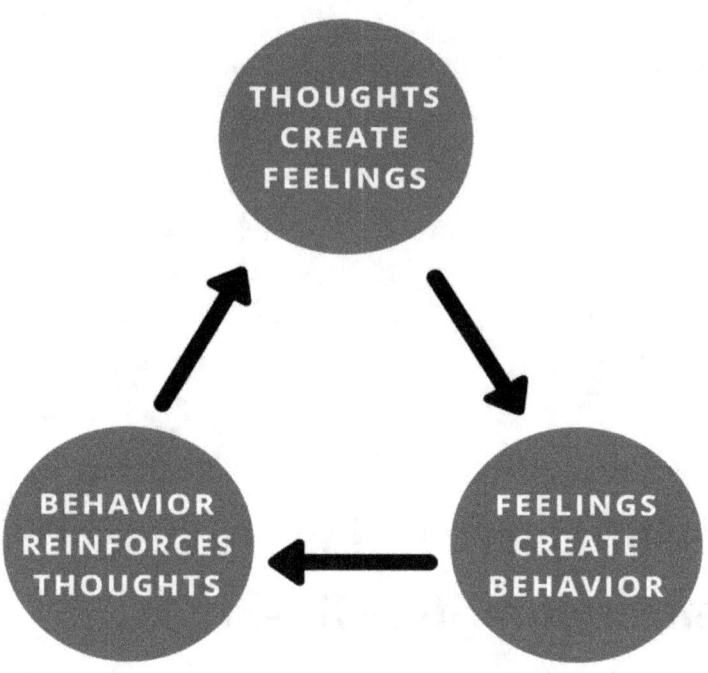

[The cognitive triangle. The top of the triangle reads "thoughts create feelings" which leads clockwise to the bottom of the triangle reading "feelings create behavior," with arrows then leading to the bottom left of the triangle reading "behavior reinforces thought," which is completed with an arrow leading back to the original position at the top of the triangle.]

By understanding how the cognitive triangle works, you can improve your mental health. For instance, you know that behavior reinforces thoughts, therefore you don't want to act on any behavior that will reinforce negative thoughts, as these negative thoughts will then worsen your feelings, and these feelings will then once again worsen your behavior. It is a vicious cycle.

Look at these two examples:

1. You wake up feeling depressed or anxious, so you say, "I FEEL TOO BAD TODAY, I'LL SKIP MY THERAPY TODAY AND JUST DO IT TOMORROW INSTEAD."

2. While you feel depressed or anxious, you understand the importance of therapy, saying "YES, I DON'T FEEL LIKE DOING MY THERAPY, BUT IT WILL PROBABLY MAKE ME FEEL BETTER. I'M GOING TO DO IT."

By choosing the second option you will be breaking the cycle of depression/anxiety and choosing to improve your mental health.

At the beginning of therapy, it is important to set goals to help you decide where you want to get, as you can't arrive at a location *if you don't first know your destination*. Customize these goals to fit your specific situation, as everyone will have their own goals. For instance, one person might have the goal to reduce suicidal ideation whereas another person may want to reduce their social anxiety by fifty percent. Use these goals as guidelines and then customize them to fit your needs:

1. Reduce the feelings of depression/anxiety by 50%

2. Reduce the amount of time I am depressed/anxious by 50%

3. Learn ways to prevent bouts of depression/anxiety

4. Feel more in control of my life

You should also learn what your specific symptoms of depression and anxiety are. Following we will list some of the most common symptoms. You should make your own list of whichever of these symptoms you experience. Keep in mind that you don't have to experience all of these symptoms to be diagnosed with either of these disorders, as symptoms will vary from person to person.

Depression Symptoms:

- Feelings of hopelessness and helplessness

- Lack of interest in daily activities, hobbies, or favorite past times
- Changes in sleep, appetite, or weight
- Loss of energy
- Anger, irritability, or frustration
- Self-loathing
- Concentration difficulties
- Reckless behavior
- Unexplained pains and aches
- Feelings of emptiness, numbness, sadness, or tearfulness
- Restlessness or agitation
- Slowed body movements, thinking, or speaking
- Feelings of guilt, worthlessness, or self-blame
- Memory loss
- Self-harm or thoughts of self-harm
- Thoughts of death, suicidal thoughts, or suicidal attempts

If you suspect you have depression please contact your doctor right away, as you may need medical intervention. While CBT is a great treatment option for depression, some people need medication as well due to an imbalance in hormones or other physical causes.

Now that you know the symptoms of depression, let's have a look at the most common symptoms of anxiety. Please keep in mind that there are many types of anxiety disorders, so these symptoms vary greatly from person to person depending on the type of anxiety disorder they have. Some of the more common types of anxiety disorders include generalized anxiety disorder, social anxiety disorder, panic disorder, post-traumatic stress disorder, obsessive-compulsive disorder, phobias, separation anxiety disorder, and agoraphobia.

Anxiety Symptoms:

- Feelings of restlessness, nervousness, and tenseness
- Sense of impending doom, danger, or panic
- Elevated heart rate or palpitations
- Excessive sweating
- Rapid breathing
- Trembling
- Difficulty sleeping
- Feelings of weakness and tiredness
- Difficulty concentrating on anything other than the present worry
- Gastrointestinal problems, pain, or nausea
- Difficulty managing fears and worries
- Urge to avoid anything that triggers anxiety
- Chest pains
- Sense of choking
- Dizziness
- Feeling as if you are detached from the world
- Chills or hot flashes
- Irrational fears of dying
- Muscle tension
- Nightmares or flashbacks
- Feelings of being out of control

After you make a list of your depression and anxiety symptoms, you want to further analyze how these symptoms affect you in your daily life. Make a list of how your depression and/or anxiety affect you, including:

- What thoughts go through your mind when you are anxious or depressed?
- What do you do when you are anxious or depressed?
- How do you interact with people when anxious or depressed?
- What do you think is the cause of your anxiety or depression?

Homework:

Your homework for this week is to use the following mood scale daily. The purpose of this scale is to see how your mood changes on a day-to-day basis. Remember, never skip your homework, you must complete this scale EVERY day.

To use this mood scale, write out a list every night before you go to bed. Consider your day and the state of your mood over the day. You want to rate your day somewhere between a one and a ten. Bellow, we will explain what terrible, moderate, and great days are like so that you can rate your days accordingly. If you are struggling with rating your mood with full numbers between one and ten, try adding in half numbers. For instance, you might rate your mood three and a half instead of either three or four.

- **One**

This is the worst mood you can possibly imagine. This number is only for on the days that you imagine being the worst days of your life, therefore it will be used rarely.

- **Five**

This is a moderate day with an average mood. This is a normal day for a person when they are not depressed or anxious.

- **Ten**

The best possible mood you can imagine, this will be for the best days of your life. Therefore, just like one, it will be used rarely.

After rating your mood for the day, you will complete the homework by listing thoughts you had throughout the day. For instance, the thoughts might be "I'M WORTHLESS," or it could be "I'M NOT FEELING THE BEST, BUT I CAN GET THROUGH THIS!" By tracking your thoughts alongside your mood rating you can see how your thoughts affect your mood and behavior.

Lastly, don't forget to date your mood scale and save the results to look back at later on!

Week Two

As you have learned, thoughts affect mood. While some thoughts reduce mental struggles, others increase them. This week you will focus on how your thoughts are affecting your depression or anxiety.

What does depressed or anxious thinking look like? A depressed person may think "I'LL NEVER GET BETTER" or "I'M WORTHLESS." Anxious thinking often consists of thoughts such as "I'M GOING TO RUIN EVERYTHING" or "SOMETHING TERRIBLE WILL HAPPEN." These thought processes are inflexible and must be changed to consist of more flexible and healthy thought patterns. For instance, instead of thinking "I'LL NEVER GET BETTER", you can think "IF I DO CBT, I'M AT LEAST TRYING TO GET BETTER."

Let's look at some other examples of flexible and inflexible thinking:

- Inflexible: "I'm always a coward."

- Flexible: "I'm sometimes afraid in some situations."

- Inflexible: "I hate myself."

- Flexible: "I can learn to love myself."

- Inflexible: "Something terrible will happen."

- Flexible: "I don't know what the future holds, but I can handle it."

Now that you understand the difference inflexible and inflexible thinking, try to catch your inflexible thinking and spin it in new flexible ways. You can do this by completing a thought journal, as we describe in chapter five. Along with correcting your inflexible thoughts, also examine your negative or harmful thoughts to see if they are one of the fifteen common cognitive distortions that were described in the fifth chapter of this book.

Homework:

Continue to use the mood scale daily and keep track of your thoughts using a thought journal. Take this journal with you everywhere, and anytime you notice yourself thinking something negative or that worsens your depression and anxiety analyze it with your journal.

Week Three

This week you should start out by analyzing the past two weeks' worth of mood scale charts and thought journal entries. By doing this, you can notice patterns of negative thoughts you should avoid and positive thoughts you should focus on increasing.

You want to actively focus on increasing your positive thoughts this week. There are many things that we accomplish that nobody else notices, therefore, we must acknowledge our own hard work and praise ourselves for them. Did you do the dishes after a long day at work? Go, you! Did you take a shower even though you were having a bad day with chronic pain? You're doing amazing! Perhaps you decided to eat a healthy meal instead of junk food? You're making great progress; you should be proud of yourself!

Try writing out a list of five positive thoughts about yourself and five positive thoughts about life. For instance:

Positives About Myself:	Positives About Life:
1. I am a kind person	1. I appreciate my job
2. I am a diligent worker	2. I have the support of kind friends
3. I'm creative	
4. I go out of my way to help	3. I have reduced my debt

After writing your list, read through it and see how you feel. Do you feel more positive about yourself? It is important that you focus on stopping negative thoughts in their tracks. For instance, if you notice yourself thinking something negative you first identify the thought, tell yourself "THIS THOUGHT IS RUINING MY MOOD", and then move onto a more positive thought.

If you have a lot of struggles in life that are worrying you, then you can schedule yourself time specifically to deal with these tasks. For instance, if you have bills to pay and a difficult schedule to plan, you can set aside time to do those tasks and then put them out of your mind the remainder of the time. This allows you to have the time to complete difficult tasks, but without allowing them to ruin your entire day.

Sometimes we simply need to have a good sense of humor. Try to make light of your negative emotions by exaggerating them to a humor extent. For instance, someone who is feeling overwhelmed with anger might imagine themselves turning red with smoke coming out of their ears as if they are a cartoon figure. By trying to see the humor in every situation, we can reduce the pressure, making difficult situations more bearable.

If you are struggling with thoughts of what could possibly go wrong, allow yourself some time to truly think about it. Often times, we allow ourselves to wade in vague thoughts of trouble and failure, without any concrete thought given to it. This can give us a constant source of anxiety and depression. Instead of allowing these emotions to fester, you can face them head-on. To do this consider what the worst-case scenario might be. For instance, you might fail a test and have to retake it or study more diligently for your next test. Often times, what we fear does not have a place, in reality, so keeping what really could go wrong in mind prevents us from just running away with any fear that pops into our minds. However, when doing this, remind yourself that failure is only one possibility among many; it may never happen.

Become your own life coach by considering how you want circumstances in your life to turn out. Are your hopes realistic? What steps do you need to take to attain your goals? Recognize that by creating a plan and making goals to succeed you can help decrease your anxiety and depression.

Homework:

Continue to use the thought journal and mood scale, but also add in the ABCD method. With this method, you can control your thoughts and turn negative thought patterns into something more positive or neutral.

Let's have a look at the ABCD method:

- **A** represents the activating event, or what occurred.
- **B** is for the belief or the thoughts you are having.
- **C** represents the consequence of the thoughts, such as how it affects your mood.
- **D** is how you dispute a thought, lessening its negativity and hold over you.

Let's look at an example, in this example, you are feeling depressed because of your weight.

- **A** – "I AM OVERWEIGHT." (this is a fact)
- **B** – Thoughts I am having about A are:

"I CAN'T BE HAPPY IF I'M OVERWEIGHT."

"I'M UNATTRACTIVE. NOBODY WILL LOVE ME IF I'M FAT."

- **C** – The consequence of feeling this way is depression.
- **D** – I can dispute these thoughts with:

"I CAN LEARN TO ACCEPT MYSELF AND BECOME HAPPY, EVEN IF I AM OVERWEIGHT."

"I AM NOT UNATTRACTIVE, THAT IS ONLY UNREALISTIC BEAUTY STANDARDS PUSHED ON PEOPLE FOR DIET COMPANIES TO MAKE MORE MONEY."

"I CAN BE CURVY AND BEAUTIFUL."

"PLENTY OF PEOPLE LOVE ME, AND THE PEOPLE WHO TRULY LOVE ME WON'T CARE ABOUT MY WEIGHT."

Whenever you find yourself struggling with negative thought patterns, try using this ABCD method and see if you feel better. It might take time, but if you consistently put in the effort you will find these negative thoughts decreasing.

Week Four

Begin the fourth week by analyzing your previous weeks' worth of homework (thought journal, mood scale, ABCD method) and noticing any improvements you have made and any negative pitfalls you need to watch out for. If you are aware of your pitfalls and where you often get stuck in negativity, you can better avoid it in the future.

Consider how these common thoughts worsen a person's anxiety and depression:

- "I SHOULD DO EVERYTHING PERFECTLY."

- "I WANT EVERYONE TO LOVE ME."

- "EVERYONE SHOULD APPROVE OF ME."

- "EVERYTHING WILL BE RUINED IF I DON'T DO THIS PERFECTLY."

- "I NEED TO WORRY ABOUT BAD THINGS THAT MIGHT HAPPEN SO I CAN PREVENT THEM."

- "I CAN NEVER BE HAPPY IF SOMEONE DOES NOT LOVE ME."

- "I'M UNABLE TO CHANGE WHO I AM, I WAS RAISED THIS WAY."
- "I SHOULD BE IN CONTROL OF EVERYTHING. PEOPLE SHOULD DO WHAT I SAY."
- "I HAVE TO BE SAD WHEN PEOPLE I LOVE ARE HAVING A HARD TIME."
- "I KNOW I'LL MESS UP; I CAN'T DO ANYTHING RIGHT."
- "I'LL NEVER FEEL NORMAL, I'LL ALWAYS FEEL THIS WAY."

These are all negative or untrue thoughts that increase depression and anxiety. Keep an eye out for these hidden thoughts, or thoughts that are similar to these. If you find yourself thinking along these lines, use the ABCD method and then try to switch to a more positive thought pattern.

Homework:

Watch out for the negative thoughts mentioned in this chapter and continue to use the ABCD method, your thought journal, and the mood scale.

Week Five

The fewer enjoyable activities people with depression and anxiety do, the worse their mental health becomes. Once their mental health becomes worse the enjoyable activities further decrease, creating a vicious cycle.

If you are wondering if you stop doing things because you are depressed or anxious, or if you are depressed and anxious because you stopped doing things, the answer is simple. It's both.

You need to work on breaking this vicious cycle by doing enjoyable activities, even when you don't feel like it. There are many types of activities you can do to help your mental health. Consider activities that you enjoy and are either one of the following:

- Inspiring
- Relaxing
- Meaningful
- Pleasant
- Rewarding

This does not mean that enjoyable and pleasant activities have to be something special. You don't have to pay money to go out and eat, to see a movie, or to go to the museum. These can be simple everyday activities, for instance:

- Read a book
- Play a video game
- Fold origami
- Play with your pet
- Paint or draw
- Go shopping
- Window shop
- Write a gratitude journal
- Grab a cup of coffee with friends
- Do some yoga
- Walk outdoors
- Bake something delicious
- Watch a show or movie you enjoy
- Listen to music you enjoy
- Sing and dance along to the music
- Put together a jigsaw puzzle

- Paint your nails
- Take a bath
- Practice skincare
- Call or message a friend

As you can see, there are a large number of simple daily activities you can enjoy. Make your own list to keep on hand of activities specific to your interests. Your list may resemble the example given here, or it may look completely different. It does not matter, as long as it is full of activities you can enjoy on a daily basis. It can be hard to think of what activities to do when we are stressed or anxious, so it is helpful to keep this list on hand to refer back to whenever you need to complete a pleasant activity but can't think of one.

Homework:

Along with your previous techniques (ABCD method, thought journal, and mood scale) begin keeping an account of the enjoyable activities you do daily. Try to do a minimum of one enjoyable activity every day, but it is best if you can do a few activities each day.

Week Six

Analyze your past few weeks' worth of homework. See if you accomplished your previous week's homework of enjoying at least one pleasant activity (preferably more) every day. Notice which activities you were more prone to doing and which best helped your mood according to your daily mood scale and thought journal.

Look back on your previous week. What gets in the way of completing pleasant activities? Did work interfere? Family obligations? Housework? By noticing what prevents you from completing your activities you can better get around the problem and find a better time or way to enjoy your activities.

Try creating a schedule, this can be as precise or flexible as you like. With this schedule you can plan specific times to enjoy pleasant activities during the week, ensuring you have more time to enjoy them. This can be a simple five minutes to fold some origami, or an hour to go shopping. However, you don't only have to enjoy these activities when it is scheduled, you can also be spontaneous! The purpose of this is only to ensure you have enough time set aside to enjoy these activities on a daily basis.

Homework:

Continue using the techniques discussed in previous weeks. Add in a schedule for enjoying pleasant activities daily. Begin to reward yourself for hard work. If you have to do something difficult or something you don't want to do, set yourself a reward. For instance, if you have a difficult day at work tell yourself that once you accomplish it you will reward yourself with a coffee, thirty minutes to play video games, or time to paint your nails.

Week Seven

While you created some basic goals at the beginning of the first week to help you decide what you wanted to get out of CBT, it is now time to create more concrete goals. When we are depressed or anxious it is easy to lose sight of our goals, therefore it is important to write out a list of goals you hope to attain. This is more than the basic goals you created during the first week; these are more elaborate goals that you can constantly work toward in your life.

When creating goals, it is important that they are clear. Let's look at some clear versus unclear options so that you can have a better understanding.

A Unclear: Be a good musician

B Clear: Practice [insert number of hours] practicing weekly

C Unclear: Be a happy person

D Clear: Spend time doing something I enjoy

E Unclear: Be a good parent

F Clear: Spend time doing [insert activity] with my child

G Unclear: Be less depressed

H Clear: Increase pleasant activities to reduce depression

The purpose of these goals is to help you improve your depression and anxiety, which you should keep in mind when creating them. This is why all of the goals have to be so specific. While during the first week, your goals were what you hope to gain from CBT, these goals are different because they are goals to help you attain a healthier mind. For instance, this is why example D says, "spend time doing something I enjoy" rather than "bed a happy person." After all, saying you want to be happy won't help you overcome your mental health struggles, but spending more time doing pleasant activities will.

After you create your goals, you need to create a plan which will help you achieve them. You can do this by first breaking down your goals into small steps, making each step towards your ultimate goal attainable, and set aside time to work on each step.

You can better manage your time for pleasant activities, steps to reach your goals, and other tasks you have to do by writing out a to-do list. On this list, you can rank everything by priority using an A-F rating method, where A is the highest priority, and then everything else decreases in priority until you reach F.

When planning goals try to make goals that are both short-term and long-term. The short-term goals should take a maximum of six months, whereas the long-term goals will take anything longer than that.

Homework:

Complete your mood scale thought journal, ABCD method, and pleasant activities daily. Complete your list of goals and steps towards completing them.

Week Eight

When you have a mental illness such as depression or an anxiety disorder, you have to work hard to manage your reality. Your reality is made of two parts, but what are they? They are the objective world and the subjective world. In other words, the objective world is the outside world as we perceive by our senses (touch, taste, see, smell, and hear). On the other hand, the subjective world is our inside world, it is how we perceive the outside world and our five senses.

When you combine these two worlds, you get your reality - a version of reality that is unique to you. However, while this is your reality, nobody has complete control over their reality.

We can gain more control over our reality, thereby increasing our feelings of contentment and peace. This is because when you are depressed and anxious, you feel out of control; if you can gain more control over your reality you can lessen this negative feeling.

You can make alterations to the objective world by:

- Completing activities
- Making social contacts

You can make alterations to the subjective world by:

- Increasing helpful and healthy thinking
- Decreasing harmful and negative thinking

Since these activities will alter your reality, you have to be careful. For instance, if you alter your reality by thinking negative thoughts such as "I CAN'T ENJOY LIFE UNTIL MY DEPRESSION IS GONE," then you will likely complete actions that will make this statement true. On the other hand, if you say, "I CAN START ENJOYING MY LIFE NOW," you are likely to complete actions that help you reach the goal of enjoying life.

If you begin to make changes to both the objective and subjective world that promote a healthy and happy life, you're more likely to take control of your mental health and gain the confidence, control, and happiness you desire.

Homework:

Create a list of ways that you can promote your mental and physical health in both the objective and subjective worlds. Work on integrating the list into your life. Continue using the mood scale, thought journal, and ABCD method.

Week Nine

You will start out this week by going back over your first week answers to how you experience depression or anxiety and what your symptoms were. After going over the list, write out a new list of what symptoms you are still experiencing, which you are no longer experiencing, and which symptoms have become less intense. How frequently are you feeling depressed or anxious now compared to before?

This week you will focus on people and how they affect your mood. Some people have a healing effect on our mind and soul, whereas other people tend to steal all of our energy and joy. In order to improve your mental health, it is important to analyze how these people are affecting us and create strategies to cope.

If you suffer from anxiety or depression, you may have a difficult time socializing. This is partly because these two conditions make it more difficult to socialize, but also because if you lack socialization you will become more depressed and anxious. It is another common vicious cycle of mental illness. Therefore, it is important to focus on having positive social interactions, even if it isn't always easy or if you don't always feel like socializing.

If you have a small social support system of family, friends, neighbors, coworkers, and acquaintances, try to enlarge it. There are many ways you can meet new people, so try to get involved in some local activities that will allow you to make new friends. If you already have a social support system of appropriate size, then you can simply enjoy and appreciate it.

When meeting people, you can best interact without feelings of anxiety getting in the way by doing something you really enjoy. For instance, you might join a hobby group so that you can enjoy practicing your hobby with other people are also passionate about it. There will be less pressure on you to talk or make a good impression if you are busy doing a hobby.

When people are doing something that they enjoy, they are friendlier and less self-conscious, making it easier to make friends. By doing something you enjoy, you also ensure that even if you don't make a new friend, you still got to do something enjoyable.

When you hope to improve your relationships or maintain healthy relationships it is important to work on the following:

• Stay in contact. It does not have to be constant, but at least try to send a text message or call them over the phone if you haven't heard from someone in a while.

• Be the person to go out of their way and suggest meeting up for activities or to chat.

• Don't let negative thoughts get in the way, such as: "THEY'LL SAY NO," "THEY'RE ONLY SAYING 'YES' TO BE KIND," "THEY DON'T REALLY LIKE ME," or "THEY WON'T WANT TO GO OUT WITH ME AGAIN."

• Learn to set limits with others.

• Learn to be more assertive about your needs and feelings.

• Learn to distance yourself from negative and harmful relationships.

Homework:

Along with continuing to complete the thought journal, mood scale, and ABCD method also make a list of all the people in your social network. After you write out every person's name, consider your relationship with each of them in turn, judging whether it is a positive or a negative relationship. If your relationship is overall positive, you can mark the person's name with a "+," but if your relationship is more often negative with the person, mark their name with a "-."

Week Ten

In order to decrease depression and anxiety, there are three areas that you need to focus on. These include time with yourself when you are alone, time spent with others, and feeling good about what you're doing with your life.

For each of these three areas of your life you need to focus on certain aspects, which include:

- Your Feelings
- Your Thoughts
- Your Behavior
- Your Expectations

Consider your expectations. It is important to know what others might expect of you and what you expect of them in return. You don't want overly high expectations, otherwise, nobody will be able to measure up, you or them. On the other hand, you don't want overly low expectations, or else you aren't giving people a chance to prove themselves.

Behavior is important, as we communicate much more than we believe through our behavior. For instance, ninety-three percent of communication is non-verbal. This statistic combines two other statistics, which found fifty-five percent of communication is through body language and thirty-eight percent is through tone of voice. Therefore, keep the following in mind when communicating with others:

- Do you make eye contact?
- Do you smile occasionally?
- Do you look tired and worn out?
- Are you slumped over?
- Is your clothing and grooming appropriate for the situation?
- Is your speech too slow, too quick, too loud, or too soft?
- Do you show interest in what other people are saying?
- Do you criticize or ignore others?
- Do you complain frequently?

In order to better communicate with others, you first must learn to understand yourself. This will allow you to recognize how you feel; learn how to appropriately communicate your feelings; and learn the difference between being passive, assertive, and aggressive.

It is important to know how to be assertive without being aggressive. Otherwise, you will either be passive or have a difficult time communicating your feelings and needs, or you will be aggressive and trample over the feelings and needs of others. If you are able to maintain a state of being assertive, you can be a balanced between passive and aggressive, allowing you to both care for your own needs and the needs of others, simultaneously.

When you are assertive, you can freely communicate your feelings without feeling guilt. For instance, you can politely decline an invitation that you are unable to accept. If someone asks you out to dinner on a date you will be able to say "no, thank you," without feeling guilty as you are prioritizing your own needs, but you are still being kind about it.

Being passive can cause a lot of problems, and often causes people to become overwhelmed and overburdened. For example, a passive person when asked if they can volunteer might agree, feeling guilty at the mere thought of declining - even if they don't have the time and are already overwhelmed. However, a person who learns to become assertive will know that it is not fair to themselves to constantly push themselves past their limits when they are overwhelmed. Everyone needs a break from time to time.

Being assertive also allows a person to speak up for themselves if another person is being unkind, a bully, or pushing their opinions on them. While conflict is never easy, it is important that we set boundaries in our relationships and learn to speak up for our own needs. The situation will be better for everyone if you are not passively being bullied.

In order to practice being assertive, try imagining this mental exercise step-by-step:

• Imagine a scene, as if it were a memory or a movie, of you, interacting with another person.

• Imagine yourself saying something in an assertive manner.

• Imagine the response you are given.

• If you don't like the outcome of this interaction practice it again, doing this as many times as necessary until you feel comfortable with being assertive in the mental practice and happy with the outcome.

If you know someone who is assertive without being aggressive, you might try to imitate their assertiveness. It helps to have a person to use as a reference as a guide. You might even try asking friends for advice on how they are assertive.

Homework:

Continue using your thought journal, mood scale, and ABCD method daily. Consider all of the interactions you have with people this week. After writing the person's name using a "+" or "-" to indicate the specific interactions with each person as either a positive or negative experience.

Find areas in life that you can practice being assertive. See what happens - and keep on trying. It's okay if it does not always come out the way you would like, you can always try again in the future. Try asking someone in your social group if they would be willing to practice with you. While practicing with your friend you can hold mock conversations in which you have to be assertive, so that you can practice it without worrying about making mistakes. If you don't like the way you say something you can always try again without the fear of upsetting or hurting anyone, because it is all practice with fake scenarios.

Week Eleven

This week you will continue to work on your interactions with others, and to this purpose, there are multiple aspects to keep in mind. First, when you are interacting with people you should always consider how you feel when you are around them, how you act around them, and your thoughts about them. Let's analyze details about each of these three categories so that you can learn to excel in your interactions, thereby decreasing discomfort and increasing enjoyment.

Your thoughts about others:

- Do you feel intolerant of others?

- Do you have difficulty trusting others?

- Do you feel others expect too much of you?

- Are you frightened of others?

The most important thing to keep in mind is balance. You need to cautiously learn how to test your friendships with others in order to learn who you can and can't trust. This is a normal part of becoming friends with a person, and it is important as we don't want to either distrust everyone or trust everyone. Balance is key.

Your Behavior Around Others:

- How do you help people feel comfortable around you?
- How do you appear to others?

Do you act assertively when interacting with other people? Remember, when you are assertive, you are free and comfortable to share both positive and negative feelings and thoughts with others.

Your Feelings Before Being Around Others:

You want to work on changing your feelings when you are around others. To do this, ahead of time consider what you want to feel and think when you are around them.

In the same way, consider ahead of time if you want to change your behaviors in any way and how you want to change.

Your Feelings After Being Around Others:

- Learn from your experience with others.
- What feelings did you have while with others?
- What feelings are you having now after being around others?
- Do you know what made you feel either good or bad?

Homework:

Continue using your thought journal, mood scale, and ABCD method daily. Consider all of the interactions you have with people this week. After writing the person's name using a "+" or "-" to indicate the specific interactions with each person as either a positive or negative experience.

Practice changing your behavior, thoughts, or feelings while around other people.

Consider your social network. If you are having a difficult time trusting someone, would you feel comfortable telling them? Why or why not?

Week Twelve

This is the last week, therefore, you will work on a few more areas to strengthen your relationships with others. If at any point you feel like you are struggling, feel free to go back and re-read lessons of previous weeks and practice older homework. By doing this, you can continue to work on and improve your anxiety and depression. Keep in mind that we are all living and breathing people - none of us are frozen in time. Because of this, you will sometimes struggle to learn a new lesson, and that is okay. Thankfully, cognitive behavioral therapy has largely been shown to be one of the most effective treatment methods long-term, as you can continue to use the techniques and tools you have learned to benefit yourself in the future.

When we are depressed or anxious, it is easy to cut ourselves off from our social circle. However, this is not productive for your mental health. Friendships and interactions with others outside of ourselves are important for many reasons, such as:

- They can support the values you want to live by.
- They can help give you rewarding experiences.
- They can provide stability and a sense of companionship.
- They can reflect the image of yourself that you find most important.
- They can help build our confidence, image, and self-worth.

However, it is important to know that there is not necessarily anything wrong with you or others if a relationship does not work out. Sometimes friendships end without anyone being at fault. It is perfectly okay if a friendship is only temporary, you can enjoy the time you experienced the friendship and look forward to making new friends in the future.

When a relationship ends it is NOT helpful to think that there is something wrong with you or the other person. However, it IS helpful to consider the following:

- Are your interests sufficiently similar?
- Can you clearly tell each other your thoughts and feelings?
- Do you want the same things from the relationship?

Keep in mind that relationships are not a static object. They are living and breathing, just like the people that make them up. Because of this, relationships can change over time and they need regular maintenance.

When creating connections and building relationships, you will want to consider if the relationship is worth it. What does this mean? Sometimes we are too different from another person. For instance, maybe you met someone who is nice, but you don't share any of the same interests, you have difficulty communicating, and you don't understand their thought processes. In this case, it might not be worth the emotional toll to become close friends with the person; you might remain as just acquaintances.

If a relationship requires both parties to change who they are, then it's usually better to find someone who you can be yourself with. On the other hand, if you already have a relationship with someone it is usually a good idea to try to make the relationship as good and strong as it can be.

Overall, you want to build relationships that will improve your life, not degrade it.

Part of building good relationships is active listening. In order to practice this, repeat back what a person said to you, but in your own wording. Afterward, say something to the effect of "DID I GET THAT RIGHT?" This is helpful for two reasons. First, it helps the other person to know you are paying attention. Secondly, it can decrease misunderstandings and therefore conflict. Often, people will argue without truly understanding what the other person is saying. If you can practice active listening and decrease miscommunications you can also

Homework:

Continue using your thought journal, mood scale, and ABCD method daily. Notice how interactions with people affect your mood. Continue to schedule yourself pleasant activities.

Contemplate on what you have learned over the course of the past twelve weeks, making note of the biggest lessons and most helpful advice.

Look over your progress over the past twelve weeks and reward yourself for a job well done.

If you begin to feel depressed or anxious again in the future, be sure that you are properly making use of all the techniques and tools you have learned here.

Chapter 7: 3 Alternative CBT Approaches

There are hundreds of possible psychotherapy treatment options available. However, several of these options are closely related to cognitive behavioral therapy while still having their own distinct and unique approaches. In this chapter, we will be exploring the three most common of these approaches.

Mindfulness Therapy

Also known as mindfulness-based cognitive therapy, or MBCT, this form of therapy is a form of cognitive-behavioral therapy with mindfulness practices incorporated. This might include meditation, progressive muscle relaxation, breathing exercise, and more. By using these tools, a therapist is able to help their patients learn how to overcome negative thought patterns to treat depression, anxiety, and other mental illnesses. It can be especially helpful for people with anxiety disorders who have a difficult time calming down their mind and body.

MBCT is most often used in people with depression to prevent relapse. It has been shown to greatly help people whether they are experiencing short-term or long-term major depression. Along with anxiety disorders and depression, the tools of mindfulness can also help people who are overcoming addiction. This form of therapy has even been shown to help people who have a mental illness caused by physical ailments, such as traumatic brain injury and vascular disease.

Most often MBCT is used as group therapy with a once-weekly session lasting two-hours each. This is led by the therapist in an eight-week program in which you are taught the basics of the cognition, your mental illness, and how to practice the mindfulness techniques. You will also be sent home with homework, which largely relies on the mindfulness techniques you learned in group therapy.

While a person may have their depression or anxiety disorder under control, facing great sadness or a traumatic event can be enough to cause their mental health to once again worsen. They can spiral into a terrible bout of depression or anxiety, even though it was previously controlled. With MBCT you can overcome these relapses without having to change medication or avoiding the negative aspects of life. You can do this by understanding your cognition and using mindfulness to help balance your mind and bring peace once again. Why does this help? Mindfulness practices help to rebalance the brain's neural network, thereby allowing a person to move away from negative thoughts and back to a balanced outlook. By creating a mindfulness routine, a person can then practice their exercises and techniques whenever they are feeling overwhelmed by extreme negative emotions. If the person begins to feel sad, anxious, numb, or any other emotion they can practice their mindfulness to prevent a downward spiral.

Acceptance and Commitment Therapy

Often shortened to ACT, acceptance and commitment therapy specializes in helping people accept the difficult situations in life. It is a type of mindfulness-based therapy, with the belief that you can gain well-being by overcoming negative feelings and thoughts. This type of psychotherapy has been around for a long time, but it has recently been gaining more attention. An ACT therapist will examine your behaviors and character traits to help you reduce your avoidance, which is a frequent negative coping method. Not only that, but this therapy also helps people to recognize their commitment problems that make it difficult to stick to and achieve goals.

With ACT your therapist will help you focus on:

A. Accepting your reactions and being present.

C. Choosing a valuable direction.

T. Taking action.

Life is full of changes, situations we can't control, and sadness and loss. However, it can be difficult to process these situations, as we mourn, grieve, struggle, and become frustrated. This process of emotions makes it difficult for us to move forward, as to do so we need to learn acceptance. We will only stay stuck if we allow ourselves to obsess over a situation while worrying about it. With ACT you can learn to accept reality for the benefit of your mental health and your life's goals.

There are many different acceptance strategies, such as:

- Observing your weaknesses, but also acknowledging your strengths.

- Allowing yourself to experience thoughts and emotions without impulsively acting on them.

- Acknowledging the troubles and difficulties in your life, without trying to avoid or escape it.

- Giving yourself permission to not be perfect - or even good - *at everything*.

- Realizing that you are in control of yourself. You can manage how you think and feel.

Along with acceptance, ACT also focuses on the diffusion. The diffusion process allows a person to defuse their cognition to emotionally heightened experiences. This process allows a person to realize their thoughts and feelings for what they truly are: irrational things we tell ourselves and passing sensations. By understanding that our emotions and thoughts are not necessarily true, we can defuse our emotions and think more clearly. The point of this exercise is not to avoid painful experiences, it is simply to make them manageable and giving you control over your own cognition.

There are many diffusion strategies, but some of the more popular ones include:

• Notice your body, what are you physically feeling?

• As you are experiencing negative feelings notice the way you are talking to yourself.

• How are you interpreting your experience? Are these interpretations based on reality?

• Notice what negative thoughts you are experiencing, and directly counter them with positive thoughts.

• After doing this exercise how are you feeling? Do you have a new outlook?

The treatment period of ACT is not long-term. This is a short-term therapy with the goal of helping people to understand how their verbal connections affect their thoughts and feelings. This process is known as comprehensive distancing.

Dialectical Behavior Therapy

Known as DBT, dialectical behavior therapy is often used either on its own or in conjunction with cognitive-behavioral therapy. The purpose of CBT is to help patients find new techniques and develop the skills needed to decrease conflict and better manage negative emotions. There are four key areas that DBT focuses on:

1. Mindfulness – In this area, a patient learns to become more present in the current moment and to accept their situation.

2. Distress Tolerance - A patient is taught how to better tolerate negative emotions, rather than running away from them.

3. Emotion Regulation - When a patient is experiencing extreme emotions, they are given tools and strategies to help manage these emotions to prevent them from interfering in daily life.

4. Interpersonal Effectiveness - This is a series of techniques that allows a person to better communicate with others, doing so with assertiveness to prioritize healthy relationships, honesty, and self-respect.

Originally, dialectical behavior therapy was developed for people with a borderline personality disorder, meaning that it is a great choice for those diagnosed with this condition. However, since then, it has been found that DBT can help many other conditions, as well. People with bipolar disorder, anxiety disorders, depression, post-traumatic stress disorder, eating disorders, and addictions can also benefit from this type of therapy. In short, this type of therapy is great for anyone who wishes to better handle difficult situations, control their emotions, communicate more effectively, and become more present in the current moment.

Most often, DBT therapy consists of both group and one-on-one sessions. During the individual sessions, a patient will discuss all of the needed information, plans, and any problems. Both during the individual and group sessions, the therapist will help the patient to stay motivated while learning to adopt the necessary techniques into daily life. They will also address any complications or obstacles, coming up with possible solutions for each individual.

The group therapy sessions are to allow patients to practice their skills and techniques alongside other patients. This gives all of the patient's increased moral support and encouragement, as they can all help each other along during the process. During these sessions, everyone is assigned group homework, such as mindfulness exercises and other techniques. On average, group sessions take place weekly, last for two hours each, and continue for a period of six months.

DBT was created by Dr. Marsha Linehan in the 1980s as an offshoot of cognitive behavioral therapy, specifically to treat people with a borderline personality disorder. As people with this disorder struggle with extreme emotions, they have difficulty controlling, the purpose of DBT is to help these individuals gain control. While the emotions and thoughts may be extreme and seem uncontrollable, making relationships volatile, with DBT an individual is able to learn how to manage conflict and control their emotions.

Chapter 8: Discover 7 Inspiring Tales of CBT Success

There are many reasons to use cognitive behavioral therapy to help lower your overall stress or treat depression, general anxiety disorder, social anxiety disorder, obsessive-compulsive disorder, post-traumatic stress disorder, addiction, bipolar disorder, and more. However, if you have not yet experienced these benefits for yourself it can be hard to believe. Thankfully, there have been many people who have come before you. In this chapter, we will look at some real-life stories of success gained due to CBT. Please keep in mind that the names have been changed to respect the patients' privacy.

Christine's Story

Christine felt different from everyone else around her. Of course, nobody else was like her, she was just being silly. Weak. Pathetic. That was her. Why couldn't she cope like everyone else? Everyone must get anxious from time to time, so why is it that she was the only one who was completely worthless?

At thirty-nine-years-old, she was married, in good health, and was holding down a responsible job. While she considered herself generally confident, friendly, and successful. Not only that, but she had a long track record of achieving whatever she set her mind to.

She was determined to push herself and attain her goals. Yet, she held a life-long secret.

What was her secret that she didn't want anyone to know? She had been bullied. Both physically and emotionally. This past had caused its own scars, its own pain. However, the cruelest bully by far had not been a school mate, a neighbor, a family member, or anyone else she knew. The worst of the bullies resided within her own mind as a consequence of her nearly non-existent self-esteem.

The inner bully would constantly berate her, hurling insults that hit right at her insecurities: "You're an embarrassment," "You're ridiculous," "You're weird," "You're stupid," "Nobody likes you, they don't even love you," You're not good enough." These insults, and more, chipped away on her on a daily basis.

Then, one cold evening in the middle of winter, Christine was wandering alone on the beach. As the cold wind whipped her face it stung against the tears that fell from her eyes, as she felt dead inside, completely useless and numb. Life had not been easy lately. During the past several months, she had experienced a panic attack while on the job, which left her feeling completely ill at ease and unnerved. What if it happened again? However, she had been through the worst circumstances in life, couldn't she just cope?

Well, she tried to cope. But after a few weeks, she could no longer think straight. She became confused and forgetful. Unable to sleep at night she was in a constant state of panic, feeling out of control and emotionally raw. She could no longer keep up outward appearances, as she couldn't remember her pin number and would leave the keys in the front door to her apartment. Loud noises were jarring, she couldn't handle being around other people. A single conversation with a friend or colleague would send her into a state of uncontrolled paranoia. At one point, Christine even forgot where she lived and how to drive.

She had a complete breakdown.

At this point, she felt as though she was losing her mind. She knew it was no longer something she could cope with on her own, after all, coping wasn't happening. She went to her general practitioner completely distressed and overwhelmed, which resulted in being diagnosed with generalized anxiety disorder, given an anti-anxiety medicine prescription, and requiring two weeks off of work. With the help of the medication, Christine was able to cope until she got into a therapist, who set up a six-month cognitive behavioral therapy schedule for her.

Her therapist, who specialized in CBT, helped Christine to understand what was happening and why she felt so out of control. Not only that, but her therapist also helped her to finally develop an understanding of her inner critic which was a result of unreasonable and self-imposed rules that she unintentionally created for herself over a period of many years. These rules she had formed for herself all formed due to deeply held core beliefs, which were created through her interactions in the world. These beliefs formed her cognition.

However, Christine now learned that sometimes these core beliefs are flawed, skewed, harmful, or completely wrong. They form an irrational cognition. When exploring her cognition and the beliefs it held, Christine had enlightening experiences. Although, other times it was really upsetting, as these beliefs dealt with long-buried experienced and wounds that were raw and painful. Despite some of these situations being painful, it helped her to be able to discuss and reassess the inaccuracies, allowing her to create new and healthier thoughts in their place.

With her six months of CBT therapy, Christine was able to rediscover herself, her voice, and her presence at work. No longer was she worried about any possible error she might make, obsessing over past mistakes, or over-analyzing every small detail of everything that happened to her.

While she was previously obsessed with others' opinions of herself, causing her to panic, she has now learned too not to worry about it. Feeling so liberated as to even say "SO WHAT?!" if a person holds a negative opinion or wrong idea about her.

After now finishing her CBT, Christine has made remarkable progress, however, she is still working on overcoming decades of an irrational cognition. She is still working on accepting herself as being lovable, but she can now say "I'M ALRIGHT." Social events still are a little challenging, yet she can now take compliments and positive feedback. No longer does she take everything personally. She has learned how to be open and share her heart with those around her. Instead of pretending everything is okay, she has learned when and how to ask for help.

Christine has even been open about sharing her mental health struggles with others, which have allowed them to better understand her. Moreover, this had led to more of her friends and coworkers sharing their own mental health struggles, allowing everyone to better support one another.

The difference before and after CBT is night and day, and Christine only continues to improve as she uses the tools and techniques she learned in therapy.

Sarah's Story

People were often shocked by the classic small-town feel of Sarah's hometown. Where she lived, everyone knew everybody else, no one locked their cars or even their homes, and every Friday night the whole town would go on down to the local high school to watch the football game. Growing up on a hobby farm right outside of town, she enjoyed life with her parents, who were the most generous and funny people she knew.

She was the happiest girl on earth. At least, she should have been. The truth was that there was something completely overtaking her life and stealing her joy. What was that? Undiagnosed obsessive-compulsive disorder, or OCD.

For twenty years, Sarah tried numerous failed prescriptions, experienced side effect after side effect from the list of medications and participated in countless hours of talk therapy. Her psychiatrist didn't know what else to do. Finally, after nothing else had worked, she was referred to the city to see an OCD specialist. This specialist was going to change her life, as he asked her if she wanted to try cognitive-behavioral therapy.

However, he said, "IT WILL BE HELL."

While her new OCD specialist knew that the therapy process wouldn't be easy for someone like Sarah (who was suffering from severe OCD), he believed it would be worth it. It was important that he was upfront with her so that she was prepared to get through the hard times and see the sun rise over the horizon when things started to improve.

Sarah was willing to do it. After all, daily life with OCD was already hell. She was willing to endure short-term discomfort if it meant finally getting her severe symptoms managed after over twenty years. She finally had a glimmer of hope, and she was willing to see it through.

During her first couple of weeks with her new therapist, they mostly dealt with explaining the process and going through her condition. To this end, she was asked about her specific compulsions and obsessions and what triggered them. The purpose of this was so that her therapist could later on work on using CBT-based exposure therapy. After all, he couldn't push her buttons and to trigger her compulsions if he didn't first understand them. For instance, he would say "HOW MUCH WOULD IT STRESS YOU OUT IF YOU COULDN'T [INSERT COMPULSION] AFTER [INSERT TRIGGER] HAPPENED?" While she knew answering these questions would make life difficult for a short time, she was all in and laid all her cards out on the table.

This was her last hope for a happy and normal life.

Sarah's therapist had her complete the Yale-Brown Obsessive-Compulsive Scale, which is a test that psychology professionals use to not only diagnose OCD, but also to determine what treatment is needed. Thanks to this scale, Sarah was able to learn that her case is moderate. This surprised her since it had ruined so much of her life. Although, there are people who experience this disorder to such a degree that they are unable to touch their loved ones, can't leave home, and wash their hands with pure bleach and Brillo pads.

The therapist helped her to create measurable goals for her initial treatment plan. The main two goals were:

- A fifty-percent distress reduction when focused on upsetting stimulus

- Six consecutive weeks of no rituals or avoidance

The next few months of therapy were beginning to sound very, VERY long.

Sarah's form of OCD is known as scrupulosity, meaning most of her obsessions were religion-based. For instance, this dealt with a fear of blasphemy and being condemned to hell.

Obviously, she could not be literally exposed to hell, which meant that most of her exposure therapy was imaginative. For this to happen, her therapist would begin to write a story and then it was Sarah's homework to finish the story. This story took place in the worst day she could imagine, quite literally as the story ended up taking place in hell.

After Sarah completed the story, her therapist would add his own additions to it and then record it digitally on audio. It was then Sarah's homework to listen to this eighteen-minute recording four times daily, and without acting on any of her compulsions. When listening to this, she had to record her anxiety levels when prompted. She would continue doing this until her anxiety to the audio was reduced by fifty percent from her initial reaction.

It was TERRIBLE.

Exposing herself to that recording was like torture. Her OCD was constantly being triggered, yet she wasn't allowed to do anything that would help to ease the anxiety. It made her heart race and left her sick to her stomach. She was terrified. She hated it.

While Sarah was supposed to listen to the audio four times a day, she was supposed to do it in two sittings. This means that because it is an eighteen-minute audio recording she would have to spend thirty-six minute at a time, twice a day, exposing herself to her triggers. At first, she would try to start out her morning listening to half of her audio for the day. However, before long she could no longer do this. It became overwhelming to start off her day miserable. The weight of this pressing on her first thing in the morning made it difficult to even get out of bed. Therefore, she had to switch things up and instead begin doing her exposure therapy later in the day. This helped her to no longer dread waking up.

CBT with a focus on exposure therapy felt like needless torture before long. After eight or nine weeks when nothing felt like it was improving, Sarah wanted to quit. She was frustrated, largely with her therapist, as she felt absolutely CERTAIN she couldn't accomplish what he believed. However, when she was at her lowest her therapist helped to introduce her to a tool that helped. Instead of thinking the blasphemous thoughts directly for her exposure therapy, her therapist suggested she think, "MY OBSESSIVE-COMPULSIVE DISORDER WANTS ME TO THINK [INSERT THOUGHT]." This was just what Sarah needed.

Within a week of introducing this tool that provided a way to side-step herself into exposure therapy, it began to click. One day while listening to the audio recording, what was previously a device of torture and terror, and instead she thought "THIS IS SO ANNOYING." That was it, no terror. No torture. Simple annoyance. And then, she smiled, as she realized she finally made progress.

This was only part of her six-month-long CBT experience with exposure therapy, but it was one of the most memorable. For Sarah, this was one of the hardest things she's ever had to do, however, it was still easier than living for over twenty years with unmanaged OCD. Now, years later, she only wishes she had gone through the process sooner. For the first time, her life feels as if it is her own.

David's Story

David, in his late forties, realized he was suffering from debilitating depression in December of 2015. He knew he needed helped and took a leave from work. However, after eight months on the waiting schedule with the National Health Services, it was recommended by his general practitioner that he instead try going to his local Cognitive-Behavioral Therapy clinic.

While his depression had been devastating, from the very first appointment he saw a ray of light and knew that seeking CBT was the right choice. During every appointment, his therapist was a reassuring and calming presence, which helped him better deal with his own issues.

While David was previously feeling dread and despair without any answers, he was able to finally understand his own thoughts and feelings. Not only that, but he learned how these thoughts affected his behavior, giving him a path out of the darkness. He now has an understanding and deep insight into his cognition and the problems he developed over the years. David can now even recognize destructive patterns of thinking that were only worsening his depression, behavior, and emotions.

With CBT, David now has an arsenal of techniques and tools he can use to maintain his mental health. He knows questions he can use to challenge unbalanced thinking and how to now look at situations in a new light. Together with his therapist, he developed new strategies to help in his specific situation, which helps him to reduce his symptoms of depression and hopelessness.

Before long, David's self-esteem and confidence were better than ever before. No longer is he living every day of his life miserable, wondering what the point of living is. Not only has CBT helped him greatly, but because of his experience, he even recommended the process to two close friends, who have also benefited from the therapy.

Joy's Story

During her senior year of high school, Joy began to experience severe panic attacks. Every day when she tried going into the school she would be overcome and paralyzed with these attacks, making it difficult just to breathe.

In what should have been a year of shining experiences with her friends before leaving high school, instead she was suffering from her mental health. What triggered the change? The problem was multi-faceted. First, she had been forced to undergo her studies in an extremely hot classroom for several weeks, leading to fear of it causing her to become sick. Not only that, but some kids at her school had begun to bully her, completely shattering any confidence she had. No longer could she be in a large group or crowd of people without developing a panic attack.

Thankfully, a friend of Joy's mom had heard about cognitive behavioral therapy and recommended it to her. Almost immediately after meeting her new CBT specialized therapist, Joy made a connection with him. He was able to form a trusting bond with her, allowing her to feel comfortable despite her struggles from bullying.

After completing her CBT sessions and learning new techniques and tools for her anxiety and panic attacks, Joy is once again joyful. With help from her panic diary and other techniques, she can cope with any difficult situation that arises, giving her the confidence to once again return to high school. CBT was just what she needed, and now Joy is set on a path to success as she earns her high school diploma and gets ready to move into adulthood.

John's Story

After leaving an emotionally abusive relationship, John had developed Generalized Anxiety Disorder. This disorder can affect everyone differently and was affecting John in some rather scary ways. He didn't know what was happening. All of a sudden, it seemed like his life had plummeted. He constantly became overwhelmed with fear, worried that someone would overpower him and choke the air from his lungs. To prevent mistakenly feeling as if he was choking, he had to constantly chew on mints, so he could clearly feel the air entering and leaving his lungs.

Not only that, the anxiety was making it impossible for John to use public transport, leave home alone, or eat in restaurants.

Thankfully, John decided to see a CBT specialist. His therapist soon explained that he had to stop relying on the mints, as they were only worsening his anxiety. Thankfully, in place of the mints, he was given various CBT techniques and tools in order to cope and heal.

Finally, after a few weeks of therapy John's anxiety was beginning to improve. Before long, he was even able to leave the house alone again. He was able to enjoy going out for dinner with family and friends. John got his life back again, and it was all thanks to cognitive behavioral therapy.

Tony's Story

Tony lived with severe social anxiety disorder, which his partner always helped him cope with. However, after he and his partner separated, he was left with nobody else to turn to for help.

At first, Tony made the mistake of turning to alcohol as a coping mechanism and only socializing when he could drink. However, he soon learned that this wasn't the answer, and his anxiety only grew worse.

Once alcohol didn't work, Tony decided the only choice left was to isolate himself. This also didn't work, as he became incredibly depressed from the isolation. This led him to the realization that he could not get through this on his own, he needed someone to help him heal, increase his confidence, and get him back out in the world to socialize.

Tony ended up seeing a therapist who started him on a CBT treatment plan. With his weekly sessions, homework, and new-found techniques Tony was able to find his confidence for the first time, without relying on another person. By the end of therapy, he was able to experience such a stark decrease in anxiety that he had to confidence to attend a formal-dress party and regularly go out on his own without anyone to lean on.

The difference was night and day. For the first time, Tony could fully be himself.

Tabitha's Story

After struggling under the pressure of domestic violence, Tabitha had developed post-traumatic stress disorder. This would leave her awake at night shaking with nightmares. Even during the day, she wasn't free of the nightmares, as she would experience vivid flashbacks that placed her back at the hands of her abuser.

Constantly Tabitha was being overwhelmed with anxiety and panic. She couldn't trust a soul, as it felt as if danger was right around every corner, with everyone out to get her.

Before long, Tabitha's PTSD was so severe she was unable to leave the house, see anyone, or do anything except for caring for her young children. Increasingly her depression and anxiety both worsened as the situation continued and prescribed medication had no effect.

It wasn't easy for Tabitha to go to therapy, but it was well worth it. Her life is now back on track. She can finally socialize again. She found confidence, took up volunteering, and was even able to enter a new romantic relationship.

Tabitha has the life she never thought would be possible again. She can be unapologetically herself and be a better mom to her children.

Bonus 1: Exercises and Powerful Affirmations to Regain Control over Your Life and Emotions

There are many techniques and exercises you can use to boost the CBT process and regain more control over your emotions, thoughts, behavior, and life. In this bonus chapter, we will summarize a few of the best exercises you can use to restructure your cognition and manage your life. You will also get a list of fifteen positive affirmations you can use daily or whenever you are struggling with negative thoughts.

Exposure and Response Prevention:

This technique is specifically for people with obsessive-compulsive disorder and was mentioned in Chapter 8, during Sarah's story. With this technique a person practices exposing themselves to their OCD triggers. This can be done in multiple ways, whether imagined or physical. During this process, a person will feel an excruciating urge to act with their compulsion - which they will attempt to refrain from. During or after the exposure therapy, the person will journal how the experience went, how they felt, and what thoughts they experienced. This process can be excruciating but is one of the most successful treatment methods for OCD.

Interceptive Exposure:

The purpose of this technique is to treat anxiety disorders and panic disorder. During treatment, a person will be exposed to a physical bodily sensation that elicits their anxiety or panic response. This will cause the person to experience their negative symptom, causing activation of any thoughts or beliefs they have regarding the sensation. By doing this without avoidance, the person can learn new beliefs and thoughts. For instance, they often learn to no longer fear the situation. At the very least, it should enable the person to handle the sensation with only mild discomfort. After some time with this technique, the person will learn to no longer think of the situation as dangerous, even if they dislike it.

Nightmare Exposure and Rescripting:

Nightmares can be incredibly frightening, but there are techniques to help with them. This technique helps a person to rescript their nightmares, helping to remove the fear. After experiencing a nightmare and the emotions associated with it, a patient and therapist will work together to identify how they would like to feel instead. They then work together to rescript the nightmare, creating a new image or scene to elicit the desired emotion.

Play the Script Until the End:

When a person is experiencing anxiety or fears, they often have specific circumstances that are making them uneasy. When that is the case, they can use this technique to overcome fear. With this technique, a person plays out a thought experiment in which they imagine the worst possible outcome they can think of to whatever situation they are afraid of. By allowing themselves to play out this scenario, the person is then able to realize that everything they fear is not going to occur. Even if the worst outcome does occur, they will likely realize that they will be able to manage it.

Progressive Muscle Relaxation:

This is a common technique of mindfulness, which is great for calming both the mind and body. This makes it a wonderful option for people who have an unfocused or busy mind. Best yet, you can practice this technique virtually anywhere and at almost any time. With progressive muscle relaxation, you slowly relax one group of muscles at a time, until all of the muscles in your body are in a state of relaxation. This can be done on your own, but you can also find audio and videos to guide you through the process, making it easy for even beginners to learn.

Breathing Exercises:

Another popular technique for people who practice mindfulness, breathing exercises provide many benefits. First, there are many different types of breathing exercises. This is great, as it means that everyone can find at least one type of breathing exercise that is easy for them and helps. You can learn techniques online to use on your own, or you can use audio recordings, online videos, smartphone apps, or guided imagery to walk you through the process.

By using breathing exercises, you can find peace, relaxation, balance, and rational thinking. This allows you to better use your other techniques, such as cognitive restructuring, as you will have first calmed your mind.

Anyone can benefit from breathing exercise, whether they have depression, anxiety, or are perfectly mentally healthy. Breathing exercises have many benefits, both mentally and physically, and more people should take up the practice.

Powerful Affirmations:

1. I am worthy of happiness, love, and fulfillment.

2. Every day is full of possibility and infinite potential.

3. I have had the power to build the life I desire.

4. I accept and love myself just how I am.

5. I forgive myself and offer myself compassion.

6. I am grateful for my life and all the blessings it contains.

7. I continue to evolve, learn, and grow with every passing day.

8. I surrender worries of the future, release the past, and openly receive the full experience of the present.

9. I am confident in my abilities and strong in my values.

10. I have a supportive, healthy, and positive relationships with my loved ones.

11. My life is full of passion, purpose, and meaning.

12. I attract experiences that facilitate my personal transformation and growth, serving my highest good.

13. I freely give and receive acceptance and unconditional love, both to others and myself.

14. I have all the tenacity and courage needed to overcome any challenge.

15. I am confident in my abilities, strengths, talents, and gifts.

Bonus 2: A Practical CBT Workbook to Help You Achieve Your Goals

In this chapter, you will be provided with some practical workbook pages to help you achieve your CBT goals. Along with the pages, you will be given examples as to how to fill them out, ensuring you can use them successfully and to the best of your ability.

Example: Thought and Behavior Cost/Benefit Analysis

What behavior or thought do you want to change?

There's no point in making friends, everyone will just leave me anyways.

List the costs and benefits of the behavior or thought. Next, rate the importance of each from 1-10, with 1 being "not important" and 10 being "utmost importance."

Costs:	Importance (1-10)
Self-defeating	7
Self-hatred	8
Distrust	10
Total:	

Benefits:	Importance (1-10)
None	

Total:	

After reviewing the costs/benefits, create a healthier alternative thought or behavior:

Not all friendships last, but they are worth it. By making friends, I can gain more understanding of others, myself, and develop more positive skills.

Thought and Behavior Cost/Benefit Analysis

What behavior or thought do you want to change?

List the costs and benefits of the behavior or thought. Next, rate the importance of each from 1-10, with 1 being "not important" and 10 being "utmost importance."

Costs:	Importance (1-10)
Total:	

Benefits:	Importance (1-10)

Total:	

After reviewing the costs/benefits, create a healthier alternative thought or behavior:

Example: Thought Record

Situation:	Thoughts:	Emotions:	Behaviors:	Alternate Thought:
Manager at work is angry.	I must have made a mistake. Now they'll fire me.	Sadness and anxiety	Spending time obsessing over mistakes	My manager could have been angry about anything, they are usually happy with my work, so even if I made a mistake, it isn't a big deal.

Thought Record

Situation:	Thoughts:	Emotions:	Behaviors:	Alternate Thought:

Conclusion

Getting through life with a mental illness isn't always easy, whether it is a major depressive disorder, general anxiety disorder, social anxiety disorder, obsessive-compulsive disorder, or any one of a number of other disorders. However, with cognitive-behavioral therapy, you can transform a painful and torturous life into a joyful and fulfilled life. No longer do you have to simply push through all of the negative emotions and experiences brought on through your disorder. Instead, you can transform your life with a few simple techniques and hard work.

Cognitive-behavioral therapy will take time, you can expect it to take twelve or more weeks to experience the full benefit, but it is well worth it. Studies have regularly shown that CBT is one of the most effective treatment options for both depression and anxiety, with the longest-lasting results. Medication is rarely enough on its own to control these disorders, but with the addition of CBT, you can keep your mental health in check and prevent relapses.

Before you began this book, you were likely unsure, afraid, and at your wits end. Yet, you now have all the answers you need to regain your mental health and take control of your life. You can begin to enjoy life, smile, and laugh again, no longer having depressing and anxious thoughts control your every move. All you have to do is begin. Don't wait. Begin week one now, and in twelve short weeks, you will be in a better place. You can be happy again. You can feel like yourself again.

www.ingramcontent.com/pod-product-compliance
Lightning Source LLC
Chambersburg PA
CDIIW070047230426
43661CB00005B/805